Exalted

"Weaving together her own biblical roots and personal stories, Sonja Corbitt skillfully brings to life the beautiful Magnificat prayer of our Blessed Mother. Each chapter invites you into the heart of Mary and to the possibility of spiritual transformation. This is a wonderful spiritual resource for all who seek to imitate Mary's song of praise by magnifying the Lord in their own life."

Mary Amore
Executive director of Mayslake Ministries

"In *Exalted*, Sonja Corbitt shows the depth of her scriptural knowledge and fruit of prayer as she meditates on Mary, who also knew the depth of God's Word. Through her personal stories, Corbitt shows us how she has lived Mary's Magnificat, invites us to make Mary's prayer our own, and encourages us to live out the prayer in our everyday lives."

Rev. Edward Looney
Author of *A Heart Like Mary's*

"Sonja Corbitt's simple yet in-depth formula for studying the scriptures will transform the way you study the Word of God. I honestly cannot wait to share her new book with my small group!"

Allison Gingras
Blogger and podcaster at *Reconciled to You*

"You will LOVE this book! It is such a beautiful reflection on Mary's Magnificat; but even more so, it is also a guide on how to live the Magnificat in your own life. Read it and proclaim the greatness of the Lord in your own life every day."

Rev. Larry Richards
Founder of The Reason for Our Hope Foundation

"Beautifully weaving together the Old and New Testaments, Corbitt's latest work shares how God transformed a woman dubious of the Blessed Mother into a devotee of Mary, full of grace. This book is a humble exploration of Mary's Magnificat and how to live our lives in ways that magnify the Lord and rejoice in God our Savior."

Elizabeth Tomlin
General counsel for the Archdiocese for the Military Services, USA

How

the Power

of the

Magnificat

Can

Transform

Us

Exalted

Mary's Song Verse by Verse

Sonja Corbitt

AVE MARIA PRESS AVE Notre Dame, Indiana

The Author is represented by Ambassador Literary Agency, Nashville, TN.

Unless otherwise noted, all scripture passages are from the *Revised Standard Version: Catholic Edition*, copyright © 1965, 1966 the Division of Christian Education of the National Council of the Churches of Christ in the United States of America. Used with permission. All rights reserved.

Passages marked NABRE are from the *New American Bible, revised edition* © 2010, 1991, 1986, 1970 Confraternity of Christian Doctrine, Washington DC. Used by permission of the copyright owner. All rights reserved. No part of the NABRE may be reproduced in any form without permission from the copyright owner.

Selected passages are from the Douay-Rheims Bible (marked DRB) or the King James Bible (marked KJB) and are in the public domain.

Passages marked CCC are from the English translation of the *Catechism of the Catholic Church* for the United States of America, copyright © 1994, United States Catholic Conference, Inc. –Libreria Editrice Vaticana. Used with permission. Published with ecclesial approval.

Nihil Obstat: Rev. Andrew J. Bulso, STL, Censor Librorum
Imprimatur: Very Rev. John J.H. Hammond, JCL, Vicar General, Diocese of Nashville
March 28, 2019

LOVE: Listen, Observe, Verbalize, and Entrust® is the author's trademarked process for reading scripture.

© 2019 by Sonja Corbitt

Founded in 1865, Ave Maria Press is a ministry of the United States Province of Holy Cross.

www.avemariapress.com

Paperback: ISBN-13 978-1-59471-899-1

E-book: ISBN-13 978-1-59471-900-4

Cover image © of "The Immaculate Conception" by Bartoloné-Esteban Murillo, photography by Ian Dagnall Computing/Alamy Stock Photo.

Cover and text design by Katherine Robinson.

Printed and bound in the United States of America.

Library of Congress Cataloging-in-Publication Data
Names: Corbitt, Sonja, author.
Title: Exalted : how the power of the Magnificat can transform us : Mary's song verse by verse / Sonja Corbitt.
Description: Notre Dame : Ave Maria Press, 2019. | Includes bibliographical references.
Identifiers: LCCN 2019022997 (print) | LCCN 2019022996 (ebook) | ISBN 9781594718991 (paperback) | ISBN 9781594719004 (ebook) | ISBN 9781594719004(ebook) | ISBN 9781594718991 (paperback)
Subjects: LCSH: Magnificat.
Classification: LCC BS2595.53 .C67 2019 (ebook) | LCC BS2595.53 (print) | DDC 226.4/06--dc23

Contents

A Little Story **ix**

1. *Blessed Is She Who Believed*
   Setting the Stage for the Magnificat **1**

2. *And Mary Said . . .*
   Declaring Your Identity in the Spirit **19**

3. *For He Has Regarded the Low Estate of His Handmaiden*
   How God Exalts the Humble **39**

4. *He . . . Has Done Great Things for Me*
   Confessing His Blessings Upon Your Life **57**

5. *His Mercy Is on Those Who Fear Him*
   Daring to Approach God's Mercy Seat **73**

6. *He Has Shown Strength with His Arm*
   God's Power in Human Weakness **89**

7. *He Has Put Down . . . and Exalted*
   Seeing the Hand of God at Work in Every
   Circumstance **105**

8. *He Has Filled the Hungry*
   God's Heart for the Empty-Handed **119**

9. *He Has Helped His Servant Israel*
   Remembering God's Merciful Gaze **141**

10. *As He Spoke to Our Fathers*
    Allowing the Word to Come Alive in Us **157**

Notes **172**

$\mathcal{A}$ Little Story

I don't know why it always surprises me that when I choose something, I often find God has also somehow chosen it for me. When I selected the Magnificat for my next *Bible Study Evangelista Show* study series, I was wading into unfamiliar territory. Mary is a familiar friend to most Catholics, but as a convert from denominationalism, I had a "Meh!" notion toward Jesus' mother.

As I began to do the research for this series, however, I found my heart slowly changing as I made a startling discovery: *No one could love Jesus' mother more than he does. And he wanted me (and he wants you) to get to know her the way he knows her.* I was humbled when this realization first hit me, because I realized he must have been a little put off by my ambivalence toward his mom! Experiencing her gentle "motherliness" has been a profound and beautiful gift.

I can't wait to share more of my story with you. For now, I'll say this: Mary was (and is) not who I imagined, some quiet, shy, naïve teenager who stumbled into the Virgin birth as though she fell into a rain puddle. She *was made* for it—and for him. And she had to be fierce to mother him.

Even now, Mary retains her utter uniqueness, because she alone can be at the same time mother and disciple of the Lord. When we draw close to her and enter into her yes as fellow Christians, we allow her to gather us up in her motherly mantle. We are pulled up into the communion of love—like a big hug—communicated through the man who "gave himself up for her" (Eph 5:25) and for each of us, even unto death on a cross.

Though I was unaware of it when I first began this study, I came to see the Magnificat as a personal gift from Jesus, preserved for us by the Holy Spirit for millennia: this ancient canticle shows us the many ways that Jesus' mother Mary is a very special gift from him to the whole church.

Hear the Heartbeat of the Church

I like to tell people that I offer "Bible study spinach that tastes like cake." Mary's joyful response to the revelation of the Incarnation, recorded in Luke's gospel, is the heartbeat of the liturgical and devotional life of the Church, revealed in both the Rosary (in the Annunciation and Visitation Mysteries) and daily office (at Vespers).

While the Magnificat's origins have been the subject of academic debate, Mary approaches us as a mother, not an academic. Therefore, our exploration of the Magnificat will be more meditative than critical. We approach Mary as an icon of every soul seeking its relationship to God and see that she invites us to a particular relationship with the Holy Spirit that is revealed through her song. As such, I think you might find studying her Magnificat with me to be as nourishing as spinach and maybe even as tasty as cake.

Whether you are reading *Exalted* on your own or as part of a group, this book is similar in format to all my previous studies: full of scripture *and* study, it's perfect for individuals *and* groups, whether you are engaging this material on your own or with others. I invite you now to consider marking your book as you read and to make notes in a journal of some sort as you go. Perhaps more importantly, I hope you will read with a Bible close by so you can underline or highlight verses that leap off the page at you, if you are amenable to doing so.

Expect each chapter to include the following:

- A Review: "Repetition is the mother of learning," as they say, so we spend some time revisiting each chapter in a concise way.
- An Invitation: This section applies the scriptures and the chapter to our own lives.
- A God Prompt: Here I offer a LOVE the Word scripture exercise to help you get personally and directly in touch with God. Each exercise targets a particular type of personality or temperament, so you might find yourself drawn to some of these exercises more than others, and that's okay.

Let's Begin

Exalted breaks down the Magnificat, line by line. This ancient canticle is the fruit of Mary's prayer and a model of praise for the Church, as is illustrated in its inclusion in the daily office and at Mass. Together, verse by verse, we will explore how Mary teaches that each of us is called to be a magnificat, too: to be so fully what we were created to be that our own lives give unique witness to the power of God in the world.

Is it a surprising thought, that God desires to exalt you in a way that you were specially created for, and that can glorify him? I hope you will ponder that thought as you read. Consider that the suggestion could be a special invitation from the Holy Spirit to go deeper with him.

What if the Holy Spirit is inviting you to a more fruitful and powerful prayer life? What if this invitation involves knowing Mary in a way you never considered before? What if the nature of that invitation is contained and preserved in scripture in the words of the first person to incarnate a complete yes to him? Could her Magnificat be the key to your deepest longings and desires?

"Let it be done to me . . ." Amen. And so, let's begin.

Introductory Group Questions

If you are reading *Exalted* as part of a group, here are a few questions to keep in mind as you finish the introduction. (You can also use them as journal prompts, if you are doing the book on your own.)

- As you study the cover and title of the book, what are your impressions? What are your thoughts about Mary? Why do you think her prayers were and are so powerful?
- After you have read through the introduction together, either silently or aloud as a group, discuss: What do you hope to take away from this study? What do you want the Holy Spirit to do in your life?
- In your Bible, thumb through Luke 1 for a moment or two, paying special attention to the chapter and paragraph headings in bold print. Is there anything that strikes you about the sequence of events?
- Based on what you see in the scripture text, try to imagine Mary's relationship to the Holy Spirit. What does it suggest about the relationship between personal holiness and intimacy with the Spirit?
- Do you ever find yourself reluctant to relate to Mary as your spiritual mother? What, if anything, makes you hesitate? What makes you most uncomfortable about her? How

do you hope or anticipate your relationship with the Holy Spirit to change as you work through this book?

Conclude the session by praying the Our Father.

$\mathcal{B}$lessed Is She Who Believed

(Luke 1:45)

Setting the Stage for the Magnificat

The prayerful young peasant hugs her secret close, a secret so powerful that it has taken root inside her and become incarnate as a brand-new life. That holy moment must be an unspeakable thrill for Mary. She touches the reality timidly and turns her encounter with the angel over and over in her mind.

As the miles pass on her way through the hill country to visit Elizabeth, Mary considers the significance—and consequence—of God's invitation through the angel from every possible angle, replaying the words repeatedly, jumping up and down and twirling around in her soul until she's dizzy with the implications. As the reality of her supernatural motherhood sets in, from the angel to the Magi, she is continually "pondering . . . in her heart" (Lk 2:19).

Arriving at last at the home of Elizabeth and Zechariah, Mary embraces her cousin, who reveals that she too knows and understands and *believes* the unspeakable thing that has happened. "Blessed is she who believed," Elizabeth says to her, affirming at once the fulfillment of her own dreams *and* those of Mary (Lk 1:45). Both their longings have been miraculously answered.

This was the moment, the cosmic set-up, the *invitation*. Then and there the Spirit, who had been whispering to her all the way up into the hill country of Judea, erupted in an exalted canticle of prophecy and praise. A riot of poetry fizzed out of her, spreading out in a pool of song that ran up the sides of the hills of history like a wave. We know it now as the Magnificat, Mary's Song, which in time became the song of the Church.

> My soul magnifies the Lord,
> and my spirit rejoices in God my Savior,
> for he has regarded the low estate of his
>   handmaiden.
> For behold, henceforth all generations will
>   call me blessed;
> for he who is mighty has done great things
>   for me,
> and holy is his name.
> And his mercy is on those who fear him
> from generation to generation.
> He has shown strength with his arm,
> he has scattered the proud in the imagination
>   of their hearts,
> he has put down the mighty from their
>   thrones,
> and exalted those of low degree;
> he has filled the hungry with good things,
> and the rich he has sent empty away.

He has helped his servant Israel,
in remembrance of his mercy,
as he spoke to our fathers,
to Abraham and to his posterity for ever.
(Lk 1:46–55)

Mother of Dreams

Perhaps because of the way I was brought up, and perhaps even due to mothering my own boys, I have a deep regard for motherhood. Great mothers must be fully present; they must intuit, nurture, console, protect, direct, correct, encourage, teach, and suffer. And at times, in order to do these things, it is sometimes necessary to relinquish some of their own dreams along the way. Sometimes those dreams return to us—and sometimes they don't.

I meet people all the time who think dreams are childish, who gave up on their dream long ago, who think God forgot to give them a dream at all, or who are about to leave their dream behind because the setbacks seem continuous and overwhelming.

I find this reality deeply sad, in part because I know that many people have un- or underdeveloped, wasted potential because no one ever raises them up or encourages them to pursue what God wants most for them, what he made them for. Often this lack of support manifests itself as a kind of wall that creeps up and prevents them from growing into their fullest potential, that is, their unique way of being a magnificat. Many such individuals have never had a mother who modeled for them what it really means to "magnify the Lord." But it could be that, like Mary, your dream is meant to somehow magnify the Lord. How?

> Take delight in the LORD, and he will give you
> the desires of your heart. Commit your way to
> the LORD; trust in him, and he will act. He will
> bring forth your vindication as the light, and
> your right as the noonday. (Ps 37:4–6)

Mary shows us through her Magnificat that when a desire has been created in us by God, we can magnify him through the successive, determined acts of simple and humble trust through which he brings it to fruition in us: "Humble yourselves therefore under the mighty hand of God, that in due time he may exalt you" (1 Pt 5:6).

That pathway from humility to exaltation is every believer's mission and call. Each of us has been created to do something great for the kingdom of God. Each of us has the potential to reflect God and to bring him glory. Not only is Mary a big dreamer, she reflects and glorifies God to the nth degree, too. She "magnifies the Lord" in a way that resonates, generation after generation, through her son and through the scriptures.

She magnifies . . . because her humble faith brings forth fruit.

Mary is not alone in this, of course. The Bible reminds us, "Now faith is the assurance of things hoped for, the conviction of things not seen" (Heb 11:1).

Surely every Jewish woman in the land of Israel longed to be the chosen one, and every woman assumed the prophesied Messiah would arrive in the usual way of married men and women. If, as tradition suggests, Mary was consecrated to God and was to remain a virgin, part of that sacrifice entailed relinquishing something that was every Jewish woman's greatest hope: to be the mother of the Messiah, the savior of her people.

And yet, even as Mary relinquished that dream, God had prepared her for something greater than anything she—or anyone else—could have ever imagined: virgin motherhood. She *believed* his word to her so completely it took root within her; she gave birth to the Word in the world, and he remains forever and ever. Glorious. Marvelous. Miraculous. Breathless.

This most holy, sacred moment in human history is the Incarnation, and it is why we bow deeply during the words of the Creed in our worship liturgy: "By the power of the Holy Spirit He was born of the Virgin Mary and became man." It is the moment when Mary's Creator was conceived within her, the moment when the new covenant took flesh within Mary. It was for this reason the Church Fathers declared her *Theotokos,* meaning *God-bearer* or *Mother of God.* And so it was fitting and perfectly natural that the Gospel for which heaven had been so long preparing should break upon the world amid the harmonies of music.

Becoming Magnificat

God is calling you, too, to be a kind of magnificat. Obviously not in the same way as Mary, who was uniquely called and prepared to be the mother of the Lord. Your life should manifest God's power according to *your* calling. However, if you trust him for all things and in all things the way Mary did, he *will* exalt you, raising you up so you can thrive. The process may require that you face greater challenges than you ever guessed as you are stripped of the things that weigh you down and prevent you from following God without hindrance.

Why would we ever want to go through all it takes for God to develop all that is promising in us? Because we will never know what it means to "magnify the Lord" until we are tapping into and living from our fullest spiritual potential. God wants to do far more surprising things with your life than you might ever imagine.

Mary shows us that we do not follow God's call by walking a straight and unobstructed line; it always involves obstacles, roadblocks, and adversaries. These are part of the process of formation.

As I will share further on in the book, Mary's Magnificat showed me that as I grow in faith and become more and more the person God created me to be, I am *becoming* a magnificat. You are, too. Her song shows us what that means and how God accomplishes it in each of us. Often it begins with a dream or longing, one that has been in us for as long as we can remember, a desire of the heart (Ps 37:4) that God himself may have given us. Mary's longing was to be the mother of the Messiah.

Medieval theologian and logician St. Thomas Aquinas was also a supporter of dreams, it seems. He says magnanimity is the soul's aspiration to bigger dreams, the jewel, or "ornament of all the virtues," because the magnanimous person seeks the bigger dream, and has the courage to become worthy of it: "Magnanimity makes a man deem himself worthy of great things in consideration of the gifts he holds from God."[1]

What can Mary teach me about the magnanimity of giving birth to my own dream, about becoming a magnificat? First, Mary's Magnificat teaches me the key is intimacy with the Holy Spirit.

Intimacy with the Spirit . . .

The Magnificat is inspired by the Holy Spirit, born in the depth of Mary's heart, and leaves her lips to become a permanent testimony to the Holy Spirit's action in human lives. Mary has an utterly unique, fertile, and practical relationship with the Holy Spirit. Her union with God is so complete and full that it reaches into every part of who she is; the Holy Spirit "overshadows," overtakes, or embraces her so completely that she brings forth a physical manifestation of her union with God, a union that exceeds all imaginings.

She is actively receptive to everything the Lord offers to her at every moment of her life. She receives and ponders. She consents and cooperates. She treasures things in her heart and then expresses herself outwardly. She says yes with her spirit and becomes the Lord's handmaid and bride. She offers up her entire being, body and soul, to become the Mother of God. Over and over, her repeated yeses—with no conditions, limitations, preconceptions, or demands—open her up to newer unfathomable vistas. First, Mother of God. Then Mother of the Church. Then every single Christian's spiritual mother in Christ, in every millennia of salvation history. Ultimately, queen of apostles, angels, Christians. Queen of Heaven. Forever.

Above all, Mary's lifelong yes is a complete fullness of grace. Mary does not choose to be mother. It is the Lord who calls her. Born to bring us grace through the fruit of her womb, Mary was created by God with every perfection she possesses and displays, each given to her in order to prepare her for that lifelong yes. By God's overwhelming action she was made the participant of a grace so *full* that his gifts continue, extended through her to the whole world in every generation.

The nature and degree to which God exalted Mary was not clear to her until heaven and becomes increasingly clear to the Church as Jesus reveals her role in the millennia after her assumption. Our own exaltation will follow the same pattern. Mary was a diaper changer, laundry doer, dinner maker, religion teacher, and spouse. Mary was as normal as any of us. Her secret is that humility like hers in the context of these daily, unremarkable tasks unleashes the power of the Holy Spirit in the world.

. . . Foreshadows the Spirit's Work in Us

Although Mary occupies an utterly unique role in history, God is still at work in the world today the way he was with her: Mary reveals to every soul the receptivity and responsiveness God wants from us. In this way, she is a symbol of the whole Church. The Holy Spirit simply waits for my unconditional assent to begin developing my full potential, according to God's design. Only then am I able to see what I am capable of doing, with his help. And yet that potential will only bear fruit as long as I continue to surrender to that movement of the Spirit.

So who is the Holy Spirit to me? How do I draw close to him? Do I want to?

God created you to know and love him, as only you can, through your unique personality, temperament, events, circumstances, and duties in life. Through the Magnificat we see that those who depend solely upon themselves prevent God's action in and through them. So it's not so much "What do I want to do for God?" but "What does he want to do with me?" This last question is something we can discover only if we are intimate with the Holy Spirit in prayer.

Mary as the Model of Intimate Prayer

Bl. Anne Catherine Emmerich was the eighteenth-century German stigmatist[2] whose visions provided material for the movie *The Passion of the Christ*. In her recorded visions, it is said Mary was in her daily prayer discipline, in her private chamber, praying specifically for the Messiah, when the announcement that *she* would be the mother of the Messiah came to her through the angel.

As a faithful Jewish girl, Mary believed that every day belonged to God, and she would have participated with her family and the wider Jewish community in regular patterns of prayer—mostly with the psalms—that were observed by devout believers.[3]

But Mary's daily prayer practice was not necessarily limited to these prescribed prayers. The angel did not approach Mary simply because she was praying particular prayers at particular times. Certainly no one could have practiced the presence of God more deeply than Mary did as she went about doing menial, repetitive domestic duties. No doubt Mary contemplated him "amid the pots and pans," as St. Teresa of Avila instructed her own spiritual daughters to do.

And yet it is far more likely that the angel's word to Mary was the consummation of lifelong prayer, the fruit of the regular, sustained habit of placing herself squarely in the presence of God, where he speaks to us heart to heart.

How do we know?

The first thing the Holy Spirit offers to us about Mary in the scriptures is not the circumstances of her birth, not family details, not childhood anecdotes, but the angel's message of God's *union* with her. Just as in the Song of Songs, in which the lovers' frantic pursuit of one another finally finds consummating "peace" in an eighth chapter (Sg 8:10), Mary's contemplation ends in a unique, overshadowing unity with the Holy Spirit that inaugurates the new "eighth" era, the era of grace.

What do I mean?

Grace by the Numbers

Often when numbers are referenced in scripture, they have symbolic and sacred significance. For example, ancient Jews did not express superlatives the way we do: good, better, best. Rather, they said things three times, as in *"Holy, holy, holy,* Lord God of Hosts." Or they said King of Kings, Lord of Lords; "bone of my bones, flesh of my flesh" (Gn 2:23).

And while the number seven is associated with oath taking and covenant making (seven days of creation, seven sacraments), "eight denotes perfection and completion, for the visible world was made in seven days and the invisible kingdom of grace follows upon that."[4]

If Mary was praying specifically for the Messiah when the angel appeared, her contemplation was caught up in the consummation of the Old Testament covenant promises that gave birth to the New: the Incarnation inaugurated of the "eighth day" of redemption. Jesus affirmed this numerical symbolism by rising from the dead on the first day of a new week, the eighth day, closing out the old covenant of law and opening up a new era of grace. Is it any wonder, then, that the Spirit inspires Mary to sing a hymn of praise in the presence of Elizabeth's affirmation of such a miracle?

Mary is presented with the answer to her heart's longing for her people, the long-awaited Messiah. In response, she asks a single question, not of doubt but of possibility and potential. She gathers up her great answer and hides it in a womb of silence. She ponders.

And in answer to her prayers, the Word of God made Mary the first monstrance. Mary prays the scriptures, and through the angel she hears the Word of God. When she does finally express all that is in her heart, what comes out of her mouth is also Old Testament scripture, because her song is based on Hannah's in 1 Samuel 2. Mary teaches us that disciplined, consistent prayer with scripture invites and facilitates intimacy with the Holy Spirit and is the agent of God's most powerful action in our lives.

St. Paul Reflects on Church as Mother

Hannah's song in 1 Samuel 2:1–10 is the basis for Mary's Magnificat. Later, in the book of Galatians, the apostle Paul compares the Church as mother (Gal 4:26–27) to Sarah from the Old Testament. Both of these women, who became mothers after lifetimes of infertility, are seen to be types of Mary, whose consecrated virginity would ordinarily have caused her to remain childless. Blessed were they who believed, indeed!

> Sing, O barren one, who did not bear; break forth into singing and cry aloud, you who have not been in travail! For the children of the desolate one will be more than the children of her that is married, says the LORD. (Is 54:1)

Both Hannah and Sarah were unlikely mothers. Sarah was the mother of the Jewish people, who conceived by the promise of God and went on to become mother of all the faithful. Hannah, similarly, was a barren Jewish woman who prayed so fervently for a child that the chief priest mistook her fervor for drunkenness (see 1 Samuel 1:12–14).

Both of these barren women were prototypes of Mary; in time, the Church Fathers interpreted Mary's song, based on Hannah's, to be the fulfillment of Isaiah's prophecy (Is 54:1). In his letter to the Galatians, St. Paul uses this same passage from Isaiah to compare Sarah to the Church as a type of the heavenly Jerusalem, a free and fruitful mother (Gal 4:27). As Mary embraced Jesus, the Fathers declared, so does the Church embrace as a mother all those who embrace Christ.

For these reasons the Church has always used these passages in her worship liturgy to speak of Mary. The writings of history also see the Church in these scriptural, Marian terms. St. Ambrose (ca. AD 300) writes very beautifully on this:

> The Church is immaculate in conception, fruitful in offspring, a virgin in chastity, a mother in her family. We are born of a virgin who has been impregnated, not by a man but by the Spirit; who brings forth, not with bodily pain but with angelic rejoicing; who feeds her children with milk, not of earth but of the Apostles. She is a virgin in the Sacraments, and a mother in the virtues she produces. She is a mother to the nations, and Scripture testifies to her fruitfulness, saying: "the desolate hath many more children than she which hath an husband." Whether we interpret this of the Church among the nations, or the soul of each individual, in either case she is married to her heavenly Spouse by the word of God, without any deviation from the path of chastity.[5]

St. Jerome (ca. AD 300), too, says, in his comments on Paul's passage, "The Church, long time barren, bore no children before Christ was born of the Virgin; but when she bore to Abraham, i.e., the elect father, Christ as Isaac, the laughter of the world, whose very name spoke of heavenly mysteries, then she brought forth many children to God."[6]

Each of these passages—Sarah's account, Hannah's song, Isaiah's prophecy, the Magnificat, and Galatians—all "rejoice" in a "barren" woman who gives birth to a promise of God. Mary is the new Sarah, the new Hannah, the new Jerusalem personified. Mary is the mother of the Church.

Breaking Open the Magnificat: An Invitation to Infuse Your Prayer with Scripture

All of the passages above follow the pattern of Jewish wisdom literature, which features a kind of parallelism: the second phrase of the Magnificat repeats the first: "my soul" is paired with "my spirit." Each stanza is a couplet bursting with praise for God.

Mary's Magnificat is divided into two sections. The first is a personal reflection on what God has done for her (Lk 1:46–49); the second is a meditation of what God has done throughout salvation history (Lk 1:50–55).

Just as Mary drew from the scriptures as a springboard for her own prayer and praise, I, too, can assimilate the scriptures until they become what prophetically erupt from my heart and lips at any given moment. I can adjust my practice and spirit to the daily readings so that they get me out of myself and into the flow of what the Holy Spirit is already achieving—both in me and within the Church as a whole, which he has been building and nurturing for millennia.

Like Mary, my relationships and circumstances are addressed by his voice in the liturgical readings every day, readings chosen hundreds of years before and that the whole Church prays on any given day. The passages I read each day are being read all over the world.[7] I can know I am in the flow of what the Holy Spirit is doing by reading the daily readings of the Church. I can study scripture in depth; I can sing it, pray it, recite it, color it. But it must be *in* me if I am to be one with the Holy Spirit.

Mary knew scripture intimately. Her song is the crown of Old Testament prayer and scripture, the last of the Old Testament and the first of the New. Because Mary was the first to experience and extend salvation to the world, she is also an icon of both ancient Israel and the universal Church (see Revelation 12).

Because Mary occupies the unique position of closing out the Old Testament, inaugurating the New, and therefore somehow personifying both, her song is both historic and prophetic (or eschatological): looking first back into salvation history, then forward to what God is going to do through the child she is carrying.

As such, the Magnificat that leaped from Mary's heart and lips was inspired by the Holy Spirit and preserved for us in scripture. It's a portrait of Mary that mirrors both her soul and her personality; we see her exactly as she is, as Jesus knows her to be.

At first the words of Mary seem innocuous, ordinary. But, as with all scripture, digging down into the words and heart of Mary reveals their richness. Because Mary prayed the fixed-hour prayers of her Jewish faith, she had assimilated the Old Testament scriptures so completely that when she praised God, she did so with scripture. In essence, she prayed God's word back to him. Powerful indeed! Jesus did something similar in his frequent application of certain scriptures to his ministry and specific actions, especially the psalms he prayed from the Cross. Imagine, then, how steeping your own heart in scripture will deepen your own connection to the Spirit!

The Magnificat, from the lips of Mary herself, is the Church's earliest Marian hymn. Because it is in the Bible, it is part of the sacred tradition of the Church. Today Mary's Magnificat is lifted to God—chanted, said, or silently prayed—every day in the Divine Office at Vespers (night prayer). The Magnificat is assigned to Vespers (in the Roman rite) because the world was saved at what would become the close, or the evening, of Judaism by Mary's assent to her particular role in the divine plan of redemption.

The Magnificat wraps up every day's prayers for the Church, just as Mary wrapped up the Old Testament and began the New with her prayer and cooperation with the Holy Spirit. Mary shows me that intimacy with the Holy Spirit in prayer and scripture is the prerequisite for hearing the daily call of God in my life and understanding how to become a magnificat: discerning how I fit into his greater purpose by living out the dreams he has instilled in my own heart.

Let's Review

- *Jesus wants to share his mother* with me (from the introduction).
- Because Mary's Magnificat has been part of the Church from the beginning in the scriptures, *the Holy Spirit speaks to me* and invites me to discover my purpose through Mary and her song.
- *Mary magnified the Lord by being wholly what God created her to be.* The Magnificat was inspired by the Holy Spirit, was born in the depths of Mary's heart, and left her lips to become a permanent testimony to the Holy Spirit's action in human lives.

- *Mary is Magnificat,* and she teaches me to be a magnificat, too. *I am a magnificat by fulfilling God's purpose* for me to the fullest possible degree.
- Mary shows me that *I fulfill God's purpose for me by accepting every circumstance* as it occurs in my duties and station in life and by *remaining in intimate contact with the Holy Spirit* in scripture and prayer.
- The ancient canticle of the *Magnificat* is a powerful springboard for personal prayer.

An Invitation

Mary's Magnificat invites us to dream big with the Holy Spirit and to become a magnificat to God. Mary herself has been showing us how since before Jesus was born.[8]

Following her example, below and at the end of the remaining chapters, is a LOVE the Word scripture exercise, an exercise I have coined in which we attempt to hear God speak to us through his Word.

Let us pray.

God Prompt–LOVE the Word

L | Listen (Receive the Word.)

Reread the words of Mary's song, the Magnificat:

> And Mary said:
>   "My soul magnifies the Lord,
>   and my spirit rejoices in God my Savior,
>   for he has regarded the low estate of his
>   handmaiden.
>   For behold, henceforth all generations will
>   call me blessed;

for he who is mighty has done great things
    for me,
and holy is his name.
And his mercy is on those who fear him
from generation to generation.
He has shown strength with his arm,
he has scattered the proud in the imagination
    of their hearts,
he has put down the mighty from their
    thrones,
and exalted those of low degree;
he has filled the hungry with good things,
and the rich he has sent empty away.
He has helped his servant Israel,
in remembrance of his mercy,
as he spoke to our fathers,
to Abraham and to his posterity for ever."
    (Lk 1:46–55)

O | Observe *(Place yourself in the narrative, imagining every detail.)*

Poetry and music, like Mary's Magnificat, proceed from some sort of inspiration. Take a look at a piece of sheet music (one of my favorites is Rachmaninoff's Rhapsody on a Theme of Paganini, op. 43; Variation 18).

Look intently at it. What are your thoughts? Perhaps you'd like to listen to it on YouTube. Savor the beauty of whatever sheet music you have chosen. As you consider Mary's Magnificat and the sheet music, try to imagine the emotions and thoughts that inspired each piece.

V | *Verbalize (Pray about your thoughts and emotions.)*

Spend a few moments composing your own song to God about the blessings and wonders he has worked in your own life.

E | *Entrust (May it be done to me according to your Word!)*

Perhaps you'd like to simply rest in his presence for a moment and entrust your future to him anew.

$\mathcal{A}$nd Mary Said . . .

(Luke 1:46)

Declaring Your Identity in the Spirit

What's in a name? Perhaps you regard your own name as something arbitrary, given to you by your parents on a whim. Or maybe you are the namesake of a beloved family member and regard it as something of a badge of honor. Unlike your Confirmation name (remember how you deliberated to find just the right saint name?), the name you were given at Baptism said something about your heritage, your legacy, and your parents' dreams for the person you would one day become.

Even now, the first question in the Rite of Baptism for babies is *What name have you given this child?* Based on Old Testament belief and practice, names are carefully selected and solemnly bestowed, because they explain, in part, who a person and what a thing is:

> A name expresses a person's essence and iden-
> tity and the meaning of this person's life. . . . To
> disclose one's name is to make oneself known
> to others; in a way, it is to hand oneself over by
> becoming accessible, capable of being known
> more intimately and addressed personally.
> (CCC 203)

The relationship between a person and his name was so intimate that to be called something meant to be that something. Knowing one's name meant knowing the person behind the name.

For this reason, biblical names always *mean* something; a child's name was both a prayer and a consecration. At his circumcision, Jesus was formally blessed with the name given to him by the angel at the annunciation: Jesus, meaning *God saves* (Lk 1:31).

Who, then, is *Mary*? What does her name mean?

Ave Myrrh-ia

Mary's name comes from the same root word as that of *Miriam*, *Mara*, and *myrrh*, all from the root for "bitter." Myrrh is a balsam, harvested from trees that are scored and bled. The sap oozes from the wounds on the trees, forming "tears" that are dried in the sun and then used in medicines, anointing oils, and incense. In ancient times, myrrh was used as an embalming oil and as an opiate. It was known as a distinctly maternal oil because it was also used by midwives in childbirth for its medicinal and antiseptic properties. It remains a rare and expensive commodity today.

In the Bible, myrrh appears first in Exodus, where it was used in the holy anointing oil and incense in the Old

Testament tabernacle, where God was present in the holy of holies. Every instrument, facility, and priest of the Old Testament tabernacle was anointed with this sacred oil, of which myrrh was a main ingredient.

Additionally, myrrh was also primary in the tabernacle incense that burned perpetually on the altar, just in front of the holy of holies where God's presence rested in the cloud. God the Father, then, was deliberately awash in myrrh. And though its roots were bitter, this fragrant oil, mixed with spices according to God's divinely mandated recipe (see Exodus 30:22–29), consecrated everyone and everything that touched it, making it all sacred and belonging to God alone.

The name *Mary* then—like the derivations Miriam and Mara—has great significance. Each of these women were "myrrh bearers," having experienced great bitterness in sorrow and suffering. And yet their names also speak of being exalted by God beyond their circumstances, consecrated for a greater purpose. In so doing, these names give us clues to Mary's own unique identity.

Miriam the Prophetess

Early on, we see that God used Miriam to accomplish his plans for his Chosen People. As a young girl, Miriam had rescued her infant brother, Moses, in a time of Egyptian persecution when their mother placed him in a reed basket and floated him on the currents of the Nile River toward Pharaoh's daughter. Miriam and her mother were the chief Hebrew midwives.[1] Miriam brought Pharaoh's daughter to her mother so that Moses's own mother could be his nursemaid.

After the exodus, Miriam led the Israelites in a hymn of worship at the parting of the Red Sea (see Exodus

15:20–21). In another type of refreshment, this time literal rather than spiritual, the water from the rock that followed the Jewish people on their wanderings was known as Miriam's Well. This rolling rock provided fresh water in the desert not only for the millions of people but also for their cattle and sheep and then later for the tabernacle laver. It is said that it dried up after she died, at which time the people feared they might thirst to death and murmured against Moses. In frustration Moses struck the rock, and water gushed forth again. Miriam, then, seems to have occupied an integral role in the refreshment of God's people.

As a highly regarded prophetess from a young age, Miriam enjoyed a certain influence and status in the Israelite camp. She spoke authoritatively from God and is listed in scripture with her brothers, Moses and Aaron (see Micah 6:4). With them, she occupied the highest roles of leadership in Israel.

Neither she nor Aaron was ever Moses's equal in intimacy or authority with God, and that fact evidently rankled the older sister. Miriam is listed as the first guilty party (see Numbers 12:1) and received the full correction of God, implying that she was the instigator of their rebellion, when, not long into their exodus to the Promised Land, Miriam and Aaron "spoke against Moses" over a Cushite woman Moses married in Egypt (see Numbers 12).

Miriam seems to have been discontent with her privileged position. Just as the "common priesthood" would rise up against Moses and Aaron later and claim equal authority with them (see Numbers 16–17), in pride, Miriam asserted equal rights and convinced Aaron to go along: "Has the LORD indeed spoken only though Moses? Has he not spoken through us also?" The verse ends ominously with the words, "And the LORD heard it" (Nm 12:2).

"Suddenly," God descended in the cloud and called Miriam and Aaron forward: "Come out . . . to the tent of meeting" (Nm 12:4, NABRE).

Miriam's judgment is recorded in Numbers 12:6–8. When God withdrew in the cloud, Miriam was found with leprosy and formally expelled from the camp for seven days as unclean, even after her horrified brothers interceded on her behalf. After seven days it seems God relented and her health was mercifully restored to her. And in the end, her sins do not define her legacy: Miriam remained afterward in high regard throughout Jewish history.

And yet through Mary (the "new Miriam") God shows that the rebellious one[2] does not get the last word in this prophetic regard. He raises up Mary as that pure, prophetic voice: Mary does not assert; she assents, as we see at the wedding in Cana. She does not exalt herself; she fully accepts and works within her duties and station, and in that humility, God exalts her. Mary is a woman of true power through the fullness of her humility.

Mara the Bitter

We gain still more insight about Mary and her mission from the story of Ruth and her mother-in-law, Naomi. Naomi, her husband, and her sons fled famine in their homeland, moving to Moab in order to survive. After losing both her husband and sons while living in Moab, Naomi returned to her hometown of Bethlehem after ten years had passed. As she entered her hometown with her daughter-in-law Ruth, Naomi brushed aside the excited greetings of the women, asking them to call her not Naomi (meaning "pleasant") but Mara (meaning "bitter"), saying, "For the Almighty has dealt very bitterly with me" (Ru 1:20).

This bitterness was tied deeply to the sufferings that Naomi had experienced and the grief that still weighed upon her heart. Yet this, too, was part of God's plan for her, compelling her to return with the future ancestor of the Messiah to the place where his purposes could be fulfilled. It was bitterly painful—and yet necessary for the fulfillment of God's purposes.

Making the Bitter Sweet

Mary shares in Miriam's and Mara's bitterness through her name. Their names and roles in the history of God's people foreshadow her own. Over and over in the life of Mary, this sign of anointing, the very mention of myrrh, hints of the bitter suffering that was in store for her. But unlike them, Mary received her suffering as a precious gift, because the object of her suffering was her son. In receiving him, her bitterness was transformed, exalted with his suffering. As such, she shares a particularly intimate relationship with the Holy Trinity.

We explored how myrrh was used in the Old Testament tabernacle where God's presence rested in the cloud. God the Father was awash in myrrh through the incense and anointing oil that covered and enveloped every article there.

In the New Testament, myrrh was one of the gifts brought to the baby Jesus by the Magi, along with its masculine counterpart, frankincense (see Matthew 2:11). On the Cross, Jesus was offered wine mixed with myrrh to deaden his pain (which he refused; see Mark 15:23). Women used myrrh to embalm Jesus' body before burial (see John 19:39).[3] At each of the three most important moments of his life, myrrh was present with God the Son.

Later, myrrh appears as a reference to the church in Smyrna, called the "suffering church" from the root for myrrh, from which Smyrna gets its name (see Revelation 2:8). The Holy Spirit gives birth to and animates the life of every Christian and the Church as a whole (see Acts 2). And there we see the Holy Trinity in the perfection of suffering: God the Father in the Old Testament tabernacle, God the Son in the gospels, and God the Holy Spirit in the Church.

Through her willingness to share in suffering so deeply and willingly, Mary participates in God's desire to suffer for love of mankind and in his transformation of the evil and bitterness of suffering into sweet, life-giving redemption. The fullness of her unique role, her Magnificat, is intimated in her name.

Like Miriam, Mary brings refreshment and praise to God's people through her Magnificat. As the new Miriam, she was uniquely created for and models complete submission to all God allows into her life, however painful. In so doing, she transforms Mara's bitterness into the sweetness of a total, consuming love for God.

Was Mary "full of grace" because she was destined to suffer so deeply as the mother of the Lord? Myrrh remains a potent biblical symbol of purification, suffering, and death. The bitterness of the Old Testament women was redeemed by the Blessed Virgin Mary through her son. Their bitterness brought forth her sweetness. And experiencing her sweetness was an abrupt surprise for me that began with somewhat bitter musings regarding my own mother.

A Revealing Question

Studying to prepare for my series on the Magnificat for my *Bible Study Evangelista Show*, I found myself thinking a great deal about motherhood, in general, and about my relationship with my own mother, in particular. Although she is alive and well, I was disturbed by the realization that my deep love for her was not reflected in strong, vivid childhood memories. Rather, she always seems to fade into the background, taken for granted somehow. Even now I can't see her face or hear her voice clearly in my memories. I just know she was and is there, like my own breath. Her constant presence in my life, back then, is now soft around the edges and maybe a little blurry. She is more of a surrounding feeling of comfort and peace to me, as though I am still in her womb somehow.

It is not difficult to understand the reason for this bitter reality; the pain I experienced in my relationship with my father had so eclipsed my recollections of my mother, it was as though his searing presence left me too numb to feel her strongly. I have memories of her, but every valley has been lifted up, every mountain and hill made low, the crooked is straight, and the rough ways a plain, as the scriptures say (Is 40:4). All my remembrances are comfortably smooth and level and unpunctuated with sharpness or roller-coaster emotions.

I asked the Lord about this. It seemed monumentally unfair, after all. I felt her presence in the background to be a bitter disservice to her as the one constant in my young agony. *She should figure more prominently in my memory*, I thought. *Why does she seem so ambient to me?* Occasionally I fingered the veil protecting the truth, but the question remained largely unanswered for a long time.

The answer finally came to me as I was offering a Bible study called *Healing the Father Wound,* guiding students to enter into their own Gethsemanes with Jesus: retracing their stripes and wounds with him; crowning their children (including those yet to be born) with freedom and healing from generational sin patterns; carrying the crosses of predominant faults; and allowing themselves to be engulfed by the overwhelming darkness of being crucified with Christ, crying with him, *My God, my God, why have you forsaken me?*

In spiritual direction and Christian therapy, the wounded are often counseled to ask God where he was in their pain, in the times when they felt abandoned and unprotected: *Where were you, God, in that agony?*

As I continued to contemplate my relationship with my mother, I realized that I had never before asked God that question. I'm not sure why that is. Perhaps I was afraid to ask. Or maybe because I had already experienced so much healing I didn't feel the need to do so. But in that moment, as I contemplated my childhood relationships with my parents, I found it important to ask for the benefit of all those I was leading to do the same: *Where were you, Lord, in the pain?*

As soon as the prayer was out of my heart, I had an answer that would be more a gift to me than anyone else I assumed it might help: he was with me and present to me in every breath and moment, to be sure. But there was something else, a healing thought that I had never before considered. It dawned on me gradually, lapping first at my ankles, then my knees, then swirling lovingly around my waist. It healed me with every inch it rose, and suddenly I was swimming in the ocean of his mercy: *Sonja, I was with you, every second, in your mother.*

The realization that God was quietly present to me in my childhood suffering through my mother was followed by another that was just as striking. Before I was Catholic, I had never before considered that Jesus' mother, Mary, had always been quietly present to me also. Not until I studied her name in the Magnificat did I realize I was named for her: Sonja-*Marie*.

Making Mary's Presence Known

For those of us who discover her later in life, Mary often makes her presence known to us silently and slowly, emerging from the scriptures full of secrets we cannot immediately grasp. Sparing of words, except when under the inspiration of some Magnificat, she lives enveloped in a great silence that is the setting for the Incarnation and the revelation of the most Holy Trinity. The words of the angel descend upon her like a heavenly dove, drifting down into her fertile mind with a perfect, gentle ease. She conceives the Christ in her mind and cradles him in her heart, even before he is impressed in her body.

Mary's silence is the silence of the winged cherubim as they bend over the ark, contemplating and experiencing a mystery they can neither know nor tell. It is the hush inspired by a near and glorious presence until the necessary moment when, into the silence of millennia, she is called to speak the Christ. She must reveal her heart so that we can, for all time and history, know her mystery and call her blessed from generation to generation (see Luke 1:48).

How could she carry this great secret herself? And yet whom could she tell? Only after Elizabeth reveals her knowledge of Mary's role does Mary let loose the stream of praises that have burgeoned in her heart over the six days it took to travel from Nazareth, down through the southern deserts, and up to the forested hill country of Judea. She prays and ponders in secret until she speaks from the fullness of her heart a universal witness to her mission, contained in the hidden miracle that has already begun the rollback of Eve's reproach.

Her inspired psalm is an opened window, letting the music of eternity drift out even as the light pierces in, showing us the inner temple of a quiet, devout, and thoughtful soul. What a precious faith it shows that she can sing in the face of this gathering storm of suspicion and shame. She will be charged with sin, even while she is preparing the world for its Savior.

Mary begins her confession of faith with praise, as St. Basil observed, "For the Virgin, with lofty thoughts and deep penetration, contemplates the boundless mystery the further she advances, magnifying God."[4]

"My Soul Magnifies the Lord"

Her first word is *magnify.*

The Magnificat is so called because it is the first word of the song in the Latin translation, which means "to exalt, magnify, declare, proclaim, to esteem one highly." She makes her declaration in the first person: "my soul." The word is breath, spirit, or being, the part of us that proceeds directly from God, who is the source of all being: I AM WHO AM. Wholly without the stain of sin, Mary's entire being overflows in a song that magnifies the Lord. Literally speaking, a thing that seems larger under magnification. How can it be that a creature could enlarge her Creator in any way?

And yet the Holy Spirit shows us through Mary that by participation it is somehow true. Sacred psalms are not

the product of an unaided intellect. They do not material-
ize at the bidding of human will. Mary's Magnificat was
inspired by the Holy Spirit, preserved for us in his Word,
and it has been chanted daily by the Church down all the
ages since. Mary's existence, her *being*, beyond any doing,
magnifies the Lord, the might supreme above all powers.
He is her singular thought, the Alpha and Omega of her
amen. All her strength is poured into this joyful suffering, the inability to utter completely all that his grace has
poured into her.

Lord is a title used in the Old Testament in place
of YHWH, God's covenant name, forbidden as unpro-
nounceable since the second- or third-century BC. When
a Hebrew reader came to these letters, he always substi-
tuted *Adonai*, or Lord, in pronunciation.[5]

Later, Elizabeth calls Mary "the mother of my Lord"
(Lk 1:43). After Elizabeth, the apostles gave the title
"Lord" to Jesus. As the *Catechism* states, "The title 'Lord'
indicates divine sovereignty. To confess or invoke Jesus as
Lord is to believe in his divinity. 'No one can say "Jesus
is Lord" except by the Holy Spirit'" (CCC 455). Mary, the
first person to hear the revelation of the Holy Trinity, is
also the first to truly magnify him.

My Spirit Rejoices in God

Since most depictions—written or artistic—portray her as
such, I imagine many people envision Mary as perfectly
serene at all times and mostly unemotional, one way or
the other. Maybe that is so.

Yet to rejoice, by definition, means "to exult, leap,
to sing for joy." The word implies twirling and dancing,
the way David danced before the ark when bringing it to
Jerusalem (see 2 Samuel 6:14). To rejoice is to experience

intensified joy. Medieval theologian Thomas Cajetan, in his commentary on the Magnificat, wrote, "Exultation is an overflowing joy, which breaks forth . . . in the external signs of gesticulation, singing, and jubilation."[6] Overflowing, springing, bounding *joy!*

Hannah, who conceived her son Samuel after years of barrenness, knew the feeling: "My heart exults in the LORD; my strength is exalted in the LORD. My mouth derides my enemies, because I rejoice in thy salvation" (1 Sm 2:1). She rejoiced because of the miraculous help of God, just as the Blessed Virgin rejoiced in Emmanuel, the Christ (of whom Samuel was a type), by the power of the Holy Spirit.

Can you imagine how deliriously happy Mary must have been at the miraculous word of that angel as it took root in her? I wonder how many motherhood scenarios she imagined in her heart in the months before he arrived. *What would he smell like? What would he look like? What would he be like?* Did she fight heartburn and sew tiny clothes and embroider swaddling cloths?

Let's stop there for just a moment and think about it: When was the last time you felt that kind of joy, when you were so full of breathless anticipation that you could barely sleep three winks and awakened before dawn to charge into whatever the new day had in store?

For many of us, adulthood is devoid of such excitement. And yet we're supposed to be a joyful people! I remember once complaining to God about the lack of joy I felt in my life and asking him if, just one more time, he might give me that experience, the I-can't-sleep-I'm-so-excited giddiness of childhood Christmas Eves.

What followed has been a breathless discovery of his full-blown love and the desire of his heart for me through the scriptures, "faith for faith" (Rom 1:17), word upon word. I share it with you, a bit of my own little attempt to be a magnificat, throughout this book.

Mary knows. It's the Word of God that brings the crazy, twirly, fist-pumping joy. Mary's song makes it clear that she sings for happiness.

My Savior

Mary's pregnancy is the consummation of a unique faith experience; it involves the total person: body, soul, and spirit. Simultaneously, her faith experience is the culmination of the whole Old Testament understanding of God and the inauguration of the New.

All fruit is of the same nature as the tree that bears it. Jesus is the "fruit" of Mary's womb (Lk 1:42). The two, Mary and the fruit of her womb, Jesus, share their human nature, for the fruit itself proceeds from the very substance of the tree.

But while the fruit of her womb is her son, he is also her Savior (Lk 1:47). Mary, as symbol and prototype of the Church, is perfectly redeemed. One translation renders the word *savior* as "lifegiver." Mary will provide physical life; her Savior will bring eternal life *through her* and *to* her: "my Savior." In *The World's First Love*, Bishop Fulton Sheen wrote, "It may be objected: 'Our Lord is enough for me. I have no need of her.' But He needed her, whether we do or not. . . . The Blessed Mother reflects her Divine Son; without him, she is nothing. With him, she is the Mother of Men." Jesus is first her Savior, and then yours and mine, the Savior of the world. Through her Savior, Mary is most fully alive, uniquely made by him, uniquely made for him, exalted and prepared for the weight of her appointed task. The *Catechism* elaborates:

And Mary Said . . . 33

> The "splendor of an entirely unique holiness"
> by which Mary is "enriched from the first
> instant of her conception" comes wholly from
> Christ: she is "redeemed, in a more exalted
> fashion, by reason of the merits of her Son."
> The Father blessed Mary more than any other
> created person. . . .
>
> Espousing the divine will for salvation
> wholeheartedly, without a single sin to restrain
> her, she gave herself entirely to the person and
> to the work of her Son; she did so in order to
> serve the mystery of redemption with him and
> dependent on him, by God's grace. (CCC 492,
> 494)

The Incarnation of the Word was the greatest of all the works of God, uniting heaven to earth and God to man, a divine person in a human womb, such that the integrity of each nature, human and divine, was wholly preserved. Mary reminds us that God is our Savior, our *lifegiver*. We do not have to redeem ourselves. There is no such thing as a hopeless situation anymore: "The wages of sin is death, but the gift of God is eternal life in Christ Jesus our Lord" (Rom 6:23).

The Magnificat's first stanza illustrates that Mary does not merely sing a song that magnifies the Lord. Mary "magnified" the Lord not because of the words she said or sang in praise of him but because, as her name intimates, she fulfilled God's purpose for her to the fullest possible degree *by offering a unique obedience and suffering for the redemption of the human race.* Mary is the sacred myrrh bearer. When God looked out over the millennia for one who could imitate and receive his suffering love, he found no one. Not a single person was capable of such humility. So he *made* one for himself. In her role, Mary helps me obey and offer up my own suffering for the good of others.

The Magnificat reaches out to both past and future; it is retrospective and prophetic. Her song not only rejoices in the birth of Christ but also the birth of a new life-bearing people whose life will be centered on the *lifegiving* Savior. Unhindered by sin, Mary evolved completely into the person God created her to be, and in so doing, her whole life magnified the Lord.

To believe God is able to do the impossible with Mary, but not yourself, would be to put yourself beyond the Word of God (see Luke 1:37).

Let's Review

- In the Bible, a child's name was both a prayer and consecration. So *Mary's name reveals something important about her.* It speaks to her identity.
- Mary is the new Miriam; she redeemed Miriam's rebellion and *was exalted through an acceptance of the ordinariness of a motherly role.*
- Mary is the new Mara who willingly accepted and *was exalted through the unique sufferings of her duties and station in life.*
- *Mary's name expresses her unique intimacy with the Most Holy Trinity* through the sacrificial suffering of humility.
- As Our Lord's mother and mother of the Church, *Mary is quietly present* as mother to every Christian.
- *Mary's Magnificat is the key to her unique joy.* Her joy, like ours, is the consummation of a unique faith experience that involves the total person.

An Invitation

As I said earlier, I had head knowledge of Mary long before the heart knowledge followed. But once she began to reveal herself to me and offer herself as a friend and mother to me through her Magnificat, certain teachings on her gained light for me, too, prompting me to consider ways God might be calling me to imitate her.

For instance, "St. Irenaeus says, 'Being obedient she became the cause of salvation for herself and for the whole human race.' Hence not a few of the early Fathers gladly assert . . . : 'The knot of Eve's disobedience was untied by Mary's obedience: what the virgin Eve bound through her disbelief, Mary loosened by her faith.' Comparing her with Eve, they call Mary 'the Mother of the living' and frequently claim: 'Death through Eve, life through Mary'" (CCC 494).

How do my distrust, disobedience, and disbelief bring death in my relationships and circumstances? How can my trust, obedience, and faith also "bring life" to others? How can yours? Let us pray.

God Prompt–LOVE the Word

L | *Listen*

"In those days Mary arose and went with haste into the hill country, to a city of Judah"(Lk 1:39).

O | *Observe*

Dawn has not yet arrived, but the sky over the mountain is burgeoning with light, cast in the color scale as though from a prism. Mary picks her way among the stones that

litter thick beds of fern and pine needles, under a verdant
cathedral of trees, up the steep incline toward her cousin,
Elizabeth. Though it is early, she wipes the tickle of a
sweat bead off her face with a veil that does not hide her
coltish frame.

She has walked south for five days, through sand
and burnt grass, anticipating the plunge upward, into
the dark forests of Judea. They reached the stream at the
base of the mountain late last evening, and this morning
she left her escorts behind for some privacy and quiet in
the thick, enclosing vegetation. She knows they will catch
up with her soon, but she feels the emotion swelling and
wants to get away to finally weep and weep at the terrifying sweetness.

Behind her, waves of mountains stretch, their tops
clothed in fog. Before her, the whole side of the mountain
is in her face. All she sees from her perch is vast green for-
est. Its breath smells like earth, fir, and pine, and it swirls
in a whisper of damp mist around her. With a deep sigh,
she leans into the breathlessness of her Lord's almost-tan-
gible presence. She remembers that presence in the room
with her, after her prayers just days ago, and shivers.

She prayed.

And he arrived.

Tears spring to her eyes because something
happened.

She? The Messiah's mother? The long-anticipated
Savior of her people is to be her very own son? Yeshua.
"Salvation." As early as she can remember, she longed to
be a mother, pretending with her doll until it fell apart
with her loving. Every girl she knows hopes to be the
mother of Messiah. But she gave that longing up with
her vow,[7] a vow of purity that she cherishes for its gift to
her beloved Lord. How tender that he would receive her

gift to him and still devise a way to give her the desire of her heart. The tears fall as freely as her steps up the steep incline.

Ah, Lord, you are truly worthy of my praise and worship. How mighty are your thoughts and ways toward our smallness. My soul is singing to you, for you are my joy! For you my heart is glad and sings everlasting songs!

The euphoric wind swirls in the treetops and flaps her tunic around her ankles. She stoops to finger an oddly out-of-place lupin flower, but all she sees is the inscrutability of being chosen for this monumental task. The wonder. The shock. Did she hear correctly?

A shiver sneaks over her at recalling the youth who appeared in her cave as she was at prayer. Her fear at the suddenness. His disturbing greeting. An angel? She remembers praying, in fact, for the Messiah. How glorious and marvelous that God might answer her prayer, somehow, through her vow of virginity. What does it mean? How will it happen? A son. What will he look like? What will be his favorite food? Is she fit to be a mother? Is she ready? How will she tell Joseph? What will he think? What will he do?

Lord, you know my heart, how badly I want to be a good and loving and godly parent. Thank you for trusting me with this new life. Thank you that he is a part of your plan and purpose for your people, for me! Please watch over everything carefully as you knit his parts and soul and personality together. I pray he will be healthy, that he would have a teachable spirit and that I would guide him to you always. Help Joseph and I to draw closer to each other and closer to you at this miraculous and blessed time. Help me to be a good steward of him and all you have entrusted to me.

The wide-open silence is so penetrating she hears her heart throbbing away with exertion and apprehension. A partridge waddles out from under a fern with a coo and trains one eye on her. Mary smiles in understanding when she squats to put out her hand and it trusts her to touch it. *Yes, Lord. I confess I am afraid of Joseph's reaction, but my heart is ready Lord. My heart is ready. Make us ready.*

V | Verbalize

Dear Jesus, I long for your touch. I am straining toward you. I worry my desires are too big, too impractical to be doable. Forgive me for believing that anything is impossible for you.

How puzzling, how profound, that you revel in choosing the lowest to exalt the highest. A peasant, now a queen. Remind me of this unobtrusive girl when I feel too small to be of use to you or your people. Help me imagine her secret fullness of those first days, in sharing her thoughts and fears and joy with you only.

I confess I am too conditioned by the world's methods to recognize the value of humility. May I recall that you reserve your greatest gifts for those who risk giving themselves completely away to you. And when I pray so persistently and fervently, may I consider that you may desire to grant my request with me. Help me understand all that you are using Mary to teach me.

E | Entrust

Perhaps you want to waddle out from under your protective fern and allow the Lord to hold you with love.

3

*F*or He Has Regarded the Low Estate of His Handmaiden

How God Exalts the Humble

Every time I played pretend as a child, I imagined I was a teacher. I spent inordinate amounts of time writing out lessons and lesson plans, ordering my playmate-minions to write papers that I could grade, and dreaming of the books and curricula I would one day write.

Problem was, I knew fairly early that I lacked the temperament to lead other peoples' children, the perseverance to see advanced degrees through, and the patience for institutional or bureaucratic red tape of any sort. I took a different path but came full circle with my teaching dreams when I co-taught my first Bible study.

Because I was merely in my midtwenties, I felt silly for even attempting to teach the Bible to anyone at all. I knew nothing about it, except that studying for classes and telling people all I discovered through my research thrilled me beyond all telling.

But as I continued to grow in this role, taking seminary classes and progressing in my own study of his Word, those efforts began to bear fruit. Before long, God began opening doors for me into public ministry—even as the classes I taught at my own church continued to fill up and grow quickly.

I just had to laugh. I was a nobody from nowhere who had fallen in love with God. Yet I could not deny that he was at work, and all I could do was sit back and watch with amazement as God brought about the crazy thing he had once given me.

I think one of the most precious realities about life with God is that throughout the Bible and salvation history when he desires to do "a new thing" (see Isaiah 43:19), he always uses some insignificant, startled human creatures, terrifying them with the exhilarating invitation to do their hearts' secret longing.

He scours them from the inside out; gouges glorious holes in their souls with his unpredictability, impossible demands, and burgeoning presence; and one day long, long after, they all find themselves blinking with stupefied wonder at what he has finally wrought: "He is your praise; he is your God, who has done for you these great and terrible things which your eyes have seen" (Dt 10:21).

So it was with Abraham, Moses, and David and with poor, plain Joachim's daughter from Nazareth whom the whole world calls Our Lady. Surely in Jerusalem there were daughters of scribes and chief priests who were rich, lovely, unvowed, young, cultured, and held in high esteem. Is it not the same today with the highborn, the daughters of kings, princes, presidents, and persons of wealth? Even in her own town of Nazareth, Mary was not the daughter of one of the chief rulers but a peasant girl, whom no one important knew or esteemed. And yet she was regarded by the One who made her powerless and poor for eternally important reasons. Her poverty was the anonymity that provided the protected space in which the Incarnation was to happen.

The biblical definition for *regard* is "to look upon, have respect for." To be regarded is to be *noticed.* "Low estate" is rank, or inferior position or place. We might say Mary was a nobody.

Perfect for a new creation, though, "for the eyes of the Lord run to and fro throughout the whole earth, to show his might in behalf of those whose heart is blameless toward him" (2 Chr 16:9). Caryll Houselander says that God "noticed" or regarded Mary because she let God have his will with her: "She was not asked to do anything herself, but to let something be done to her."[1]

Isn't this the most difficult part, not *doing* anything to make something happen? Most of us decide what we want to do or be or what we want to happen, and then we set and work toward goals that will get us there: educational goals, financial goals, career-ladder goals, health goals, and retirement goals. This is all reasonable and rational and even necessary. Yet Mary's Magnificat, here, seems to present a challenge: Who among us asks God, *first*, before all the necessary planning and doing, what he wants for us? Which of us simply serves in place with no expectation, ever, of anything else?

And even if we receive a specific word or vocation from God, who simply says "May it be done to me" without planning or setting out to make it happen or at least trying to help God make it happen? What simplicity is required for this degree of trust?

Mary's attitude is not one of laziness or passivity but intense, active faith. And yet she exhibits a discipline against action that can only be a work of grace. The only action she undertook was rushing to serve Elizabeth. Mary served God from her lack of position or resource as a "handmaiden," *without ever knowing her service was so highly esteemed by him.* She claimed nothing, pursued nothing, but left all God's gifts freely in his hands, no more than a willing servant or slave.

Here's the point: there, serving everyone around her, Mary finds herself the Mother of God, exalted above men and angels, and remains so simple and so calm that she points only to her "low estate." Mary teaches us that being exalted can be, and often is, as simple as serving in place until and unless we are called to step out into more complicated waters. Maybe I should stop the planning, stop the grasping, stop the hustling, and pray to know what God wants for me, first. This is what it means to magnify God, to count only him great, with all one's being, and lay claim to absolutely nothing else.

The Gift of Lowliness

Before Mary, there was a proto-Mary, Hannah. Hannah was also lowly, but her lowliness was an affliction (see 1 Samuel 1:11); Hannah's poverty was her childlessness in a time and culture that valued the blessing of offspring above all things. She "prayed to the Lord and wept bitterly" (1 Sm 1:10), vowing to consecrate the fruit of her prayer, her child, to God as a Nazarite should he answer her pleas for a son. Much like God "regarded" Mary's lowliness, God "remembered" Hannah (1 Sm 1:19) and granted her earnest request.

I had been listening to Christian radio for more than a year and was especially moved by the testimonies offered during the pledge drive, where the DJs claimed, "Just a dollar a day will keep us on the air." Although poor as a church mouse, I pledged a year of support, thinking I could surely put away a dollar a day, even as a stay-at-home mom.

Within a single month, I panicked as I realized there was no way I would be able to keep my commitment. I begged God for a miracle $365 windfall. But it never came. I believe strongly in the biblical mandate to keep such promises, so I threw myself on God's mercy and pleaded with him for help. I expected to win the lottery or some other such accidental answer (even though I've never even played the lottery!).

Sure enough, within the week I ran across a passage titled "The Law Concerning Vows" while studying for my weekly Bible class:

> And if she is married to a husband, while under her vows or any thoughtless utterance of her lips by which she has bound herself, and her husband hears of it, and says nothing to her on the day that he hears; then her vows shall stand, and her pledges by which she has bound herself shall stand. But if, on the day that her husband comes to hear of it, he expresses disapproval, then he shall make void her vow which was on her, and the thoughtless utterance of her lips, by which she bound herself; and the LORD will forgive her. (Nm 30:6–8)

I realize we are not "under the law," as St. Paul says (Rom 6:14), but I knew that was God's answer to my plea for rescue. Relieved unto tears, I spoke to my husband that same evening. I told him about my pledge without elaborating or stating my dilemma. As expected, he objected immediately, and I was released and therefore forgiven. Hallelujah. I called the radio station the next day and told them the entire humiliating story and made my apologies.

According to Old Testament law, Hannah's husband might have declared her vow to dedicate her son as a lifelong Nazarite in service to God a rash promise and prohibited her from fulfilling it (see Numbers 30:10–15). Mary's fiat might also have been declared rash by Joseph. That neither man did so shows their love and esteem for the women and their deep humility before God. It also illustrates the intense regard God has for lowliness. God always protects those petitions for which he inspires us to ask.

The Blessing Falls upon the Bowed Head

Before Mary's Joseph, there was Jacob's Joseph, who was thrown into a pit and sold to a caravan of foreigners by his jealous brothers, then rose to prominence in Egypt to save the family and the entire kingdom from famine. Jacob was old and dying, and he wished to bless his sons. Joseph actually received a double portion when Jacob blessed Joseph's two sons on the same level as his (Jacob's) other sons, but that's not the most interesting part of the story for me. Part of Jacob's beautiful blessing over Joseph reads,

> By God Almighty who will bless you with blessings of heaven above, blessings of the deep that couches beneath, blessings of the breasts and of the womb. The blessings of your father

> are mighty beyond the blessings of the eternal
> mountains, the bounties of the everlasting hills;
> *may they be on the head of Joseph, and on the brow*
> *of him who was separate from his brothers.* (Gn
> 49:25–26, emphasis added)

Part prophecy, part benediction, the last line of the blessing indicates that it will continually fall on Joseph's perpetually bowed head: the word *brow* literally means "crown, the part most bowed." One bows one's head in humility.

But even more spectacular is the word *separate*, as it literally means "Nazarite" and is the same root from which Nazareth proceeds. Both Josephs, Hannah's son Samuel, and later Nazarites were all *separated* from others in order to serve God's holy purposes (see Numbers 6:1–21).

As I studied this line of the Magnificat for my radio series, I was deeply affected by this mark of humility, the bowed head, as in Mary's "May it be done to me according to your word." But how to demonstrate in our day and time, outwardly, this profound inward bow to God? What sacrifice could I offer that might be a clear act of humility? What was God calling me to through Mary?

I desperately wanted to offer God something beautiful, something remotely close to the simplicity and humility Mary offers; I wanted to imitate her in some way that could also draw me closer to her, this woman I barely knew, this mother who had been invisibly present to me since my naming. And I could have never guessed in a million years what that could mean.

Meditating on Mary's bowed head always brought me back to her veil. I knew a faithful Jewish woman never would have dreamed of entering the Temple without a veil. The ancient practice was simply carried on by the

Church, as it is by Orthodox Christians and even Orthodox Jewish women today.

I confess that initially I regarded St. Paul's instruc-
tions for women to wear veils as a sign of their modesty
and submission to authority as sexist (see 1 Corinthians
11:5–16). While it is true that a veil was typical in Mary's
day and not controversial at all, I found myself gradually
being drawn to the idea of veiling as a way of identifying
with Mary in her lowliness and humility. Perhaps precisely *because* it is no longer commonly practiced, it could
be a true symbol, a real sacramental. Even so, it took me
a while to take that next step. *A church veil? Really? What
about my hair?! No one does it. It will be weird. Where do I get
one? They're ugly.*

As much as I wanted to imitate Mary, I was embarrassed at the thought of doing something so countercul-
tural. And so, ironically, my desire to offer a gesture of
true humility was put on hold as I procrastinated, too
proud to actually go through with it. I researched. I read
opinions. Strange that a little piece of fabric could provoke
such extreme controversy and emotion!

I read that veiling is especially associated with sacred
objects. In the Old Testament, Moses veiled his glowing
face after forty days of communion with God on Mt. Sinai.
Brides were traditionally veiled before the veil was lifted
in the wedding ceremony. The ark in the holy of holies,
which foreshadowed Mary herself, was veiled.

The Church continues to veil holy things. Several different types of veils are still used in the Mass, not so much
to obscure as to *depict* the mystery present. The altar, the
ciborium, the chalice, the hands of the priest carrying
the monstrance—all are vessels of life; all are veiled. The
tabernacle is a veil; behind the veil is the Body of Christ.

I too am a living tabernacle, I realized (see 1 Corinthians 6:19). As a woman, I am a vessel of life, a monstrance. Veiling, then, speaks to a kind of hiddenness that does not seek to conceal in the negative sense but rather to draw us into the depths of mystery, allowing for the mysterious to unfold.

Even Jesus, the infinite God whose glory is revealed in heaven, is "veiled" before us in the accidents of bread and wine. As one wise priest put it, "Like the effect of the virtue of modesty, by the very fact that something is hidden, it is allowed to become that which it is: mysterious and beautiful."

Why then is it the woman who is veiled? First, the woman is the model of the Church (as pointed out by St. Paul in Ephesians 5:21–33), and the Church is the mystical Body of Christ. Much like the eucharistic Body of Christ is veiled under various layers, so too is the Church, and the woman represents the Church.

Second, it is the woman who brings forth new souls, the most profound manifestation of mystery capable in the created realm (which is also why fertility is so viciously attacked). It is the woman who gives birth to a new person and thereby changes the entire created order—even the angels are not capable of such a mystery. As Christ turned his body and blood into the eucharistic food for his disciples, so too does the woman change her own body and blood into food for her infant.

We veil what is most sacred. This was a new thought for me: "It is not so much that the woman wears a veil out of respect for the Church, but rather the Church gives a veil out of respect for the woman."[2]

Part of St. Paul's reasoning for a woman's veil is "the angels" (1 Cor 11:10). Angels, holy and fallen, all understand and operate under authority. The fallen angels sinned in their unwillingness to submit to God's authority in Christ. Veiling is a way of demonstrating one's submission in the face of their rebellion, to reflect the divine invisible order and make it visible. It is also a way of respecting the presence of the holy angels, who operate in perfect authority under God, present at the divine liturgy. According to St. Paul, because a woman's hair is her glory (see 1 Corinthians 11:15), she veils it as a sign that *his* glory, not hers, is her focus in worship. In the end, that was the reality I wanted to express.

I kept returning to the church veil as a small way to imitate Mary's humility and outwardly express my own submission to God. Veiling is a beautiful devotion, like the Rosary, that has the potential to edify the entire Body of Christ by drawing attention to both the sacredness of women and the magnificence of the real presence of Christ in the Eucharist. This one small act is a sign of profound surrender to God and oneness with Our Lady.

For me, it is enough to wear a veil; I do not worry about the right colors or traditional styles. I began with a cashmere shawl someone brought back for me from the Holy Land. I had never used it, so it was consecrated as a church veil. Although I felt painfully self-conscious, my first Mass in a veil was unexpectedly poignant and private. I felt hidden, focused, and prayerful in a way I had never experienced before.

I am completely comfortable with those who veil and those who choose not to, and I understand the reasons for both views. The practice of head covering for women is a matter of ecclesiastical discipline and not divine law (*Inter Insigniores*). And yet my desire to offer a gesture of humility and love in communion with Mary found a home in my practice of veiling my head for church. And though I have since swapped out my cashmere shawl with a lightweight scarf, I find it calming. I feel more in tune with what is happening at Mass. God's presence is more vivid, close, private, and intimate.

To veil or not to veil, that is the question. However we express that desire for humility, like Mary, the most important thing is that we are always on the lookout for God, listening to him. Mary belongs to those who reflect on life from God's point of view and cherish his Word, those who let him save them, those who obey. The lowly rejoice that God has not forgotten them in their humble state but that he has stooped low into the mire of their human experience.

All Generations Will Call Me Blessed

Some Protestants claim that Catholics honor Mary too much. I know I once thought so. As I mentioned in the first chapter, I found Catholic attitudes toward Mary completely scandalous. As a convert from denominationalism, I never paid much attention to that particular line of the Magnificat, but now it leaps out at me as God's Word, seemingly a sort of command: "All generations will call me blessed"(Lk 1:48). *We should call her blessed.*

"All generations," says Cardinal Hugo, "that is, all nations of Jews and Gentiles, of men and women, of rich and poor, of angels and of men, because all through her have received a saving benefit: men have received reconciliation; angels restoration (of their numbers)."[3] Augustine speculated that the number of Christians will equal the number of fallen angels, that God redeems us to replace them. If so, it all began as Cardinal Hugo said, with a single lowly girl, obedient to a mighty miracle: the long-anticipated superabundant fulfillment of an earthly preparation.

It has been said that Catholics heed this biblical prophecy and command to call her blessed, especially, in the Rosary—which is not, as some suppose, a mindless repetition of "empty phrases" forbidden by Christ (Mt 6:7). Rather, the Rosary is "the Bible on a string," a meditation on the lives of Mary and Jesus as presented to us in the gospels.

The word *blessed* is not wishful or self-congratulatory. There is an imperative edge to the command. It is a prophetic and more-than-polite honorary term. Its meaning is rather *to bless,* or *to make blessed, to beatify.*

"All generations will call me blessed," the Bible says through the Virgin Mary. Her praise will be sung from one generation to another so that there will never be a time when she shall not be applauded. That is, it begins now and will continue throughout all generations, unto children's children.

Most Protestants understand this to simply mean that she was favored by God to be the mother of Jesus, and in its primary fulfillment this interpretation of the prophecy is true enough. Unless Mary is the mother of our Lord, as Elizabeth says, there is no reason for us to rejoice in Mary's happiness together with her on account of such incomparable favor.

Yet because prophecy always has more than one fulfillment, we are necessarily left with how Mary's prophecy is still being fulfilled. For instance, Abraham was called to be Isaac's father, but he is also the father of all those who have faith. Moses was called as prophet to God's people in Egypt, but he also became the great prophet of the whole Jewish people as well as a type of Christ. As such, Moses continues to lead us all, especially through his example preserved for us in scripture. David was called to be king for God's people, yet his kingdom lives on even now through Christ, and we are part of it. Paul was called to preach to the Gentiles, yet he preaches to us even now through his writings.

Doesn't it stand to reason, if every other biblical person's promises—Abraham, Moses, David, and Paul, for instance—were both immediate and eternally prophetic, that Mary's physical motherhood cannot be the fullest expression of her blessedness by future generations?

Mary's motherhood is not simply about the flesh and blood of nativity but of eschatology and spirit, as she is presented to us in Revelation 12. In fact, because the object of her promise is himself divine, the secondary fulfillment must also be greater, fuller, more spectacularly unexpected than any other promise ever before.

This same word *blessed* was used in patristic literature to characterize the martyrs. The highest expression of this blessedness was in the possibility of their ascension into heaven to dwell in the immediate presence of God, which is why the word is sometimes translated as "beatitude." In other words, the martyrs weren't simply blessed for having died for Christ in faith. As Tertullian said, "The blood of the martyrs is the seed of the Church." They continue to influence the Church to this day.

Surely no one in history deserves the title of white martyr the way Mary does. She is the sorrowful mother, her body and life given to accomplish God's plan to redeem all mankind, and the object of her suffering was eternal and divine. Surely her suffering continues to influence the Church to this day as well.

Did she ever ruminate over the Genesis account and get an inkling of herself as the new Eve who would at last crush the serpent's head? Did she anticipate that her yes would mean becoming the woman at the center of salvation in Genesis 3:15? God says, "I will put enmity between you and the woman, and between your seed and her seed; he shall bruise your head, and you shall bruise his heel."

Enmity is hatred. Oh, how evil hates the woman: "This passage in Genesis is called the Protoevangelium ('first gospel'): the first announcement of the Messiah and Redeemer, of a battle between the serpent and the Woman, and of the final victory of a descendant of hers. . . . Furthermore many Fathers and Doctors of the Church have seen the woman announced in the Protoevangelium as Mary, the mother of Christ, the 'new Eve'" (CCC 410–411). Satan could not have known which woman's seed would be his downfall, so the strategy became destroy them all.

But Mary was not destroyed; she was preserved. No sin clouded her vision or tainted her will. Mary's divine motherhood is not, by itself, the highest expression of her blessedness in the eyes of future generations. As the sign of the spotless, risen Church, she is the first to be wholly human but also immaculate, and assumed, body and soul. By extension, her divine motherhood becomes eternal in Christ.

In his encyclical *Redemptoris Mater,* Pope John Paul II says, as such, Mary can point out to her Son the needs of mankind and, in fact, she "has the right" to do so. Her mediation is thus in the nature of intercession: Mary intercedes for mankind as she did at Cana. And that is not all. As a mother, she also wishes the messianic power of her Son to be manifested, that salvific power of his that is meant to help man in his misfortunes, to free him from the evil that in various forms and degrees weighs heavily upon his life (RM 29).

Calling Mary blessed consists not merely in saying the words, but it is done with all one's strength and sincerity, when our hearts, moved by her low estate and God's gracious regard for her, as we have seen, rejoices in God. The fact that an archangel saluted her with "Hail, full of grace" is enough for me to know that she is worthy of at least that and probably more. Mary gave Jesus the means to save us by giving him her own flesh and body, making him human, giving him the body that would save us all. She accepted not only Jesus as her son but all men as her children through him.

Blessed Art Thou among Women

To "bless" Mary, then, is to accord her the honor that is her due and that the Bible itself gives her. "Hail, full of grace, the Lord is with you!" (Lk 1:28), said the angel to Mary. "Blessed are you among women, and blessed is the fruit of your womb!" (Lk 1:42), said Elizabeth to Mary. "Holy Mary" is the term *blessed*, meaning "beatified, holy," as we have already seen. "Mother of God" or "mother of my Lord" (Lk 1:43), said Elizabeth to Mary.

"Pray for us sinners, now and at the hour of our death. Amen." Why not?

Herein we have the whole Rosary.

The first time I prayed a Rosary I feared I was offending God by doing so. I even apologized up front just in case. By the time I was finished, I got it. We are praying the gospels. We pray by hand.

My pilgrimage to the Holy Land set my daily Rosary practice on fire, as I remember and retrace in my memory the actual physical setting of each mystery. I love to emphasize each word in turn, with each "Hail Mary," as the changing emphases illuminate different aspects of the prayer.

As a Third Order Carmelite in formation and because of my consecration to Mary, the Rosary continues to be my first daily prayer. It focuses me for deeper prayer with the scriptures; it draws me into the presence of God. I pray it as I go to sleep and first thing upon waking. When I fall asleep in her arms and neglect to finish it, I ask my guardian angel to do so for me. The Rosary is a gift to me in moments when I have no words. And it is a gift of roses to her for Jesus.

The Rosary is so powerful a prayer because it re-presents, or makes present again, the events of the gospels each time and within the context it is prayed: "For Christians, the first of books is the Gospel and the Rosary is actually the abridgment of the Gospel."[4]

Let's Review

- *God draws us into the place of lowliness, of "nobody-ness" in order to do his most important work in us*—just as he did with Mary.
- *Mary shows me God will give me the desires of my heart, too* (Ps 37:4), when I receive and obey the Word of God, holding nothing back.
- *God did not choose Mary because of her humility*; Mary was humble because God chose her. He gave her the "gift of lowliness," and he offers it to us.
- *Those who depend on themselves prevent God's action in and through them*, but humility like Mary's unleashes the graces of the Holy Spirit into the world.
- The question is not what I want to do for God, but *what does God want to do through me?*
- *In the maternity of Mary, she intercedes for us just as she did at Cana*. In so doing, she reveals the salvific, messianic power of her Son to the world.
- *Praying the Rosary obeys the biblical mandate* to call Mary blessed.

- *The Rosary is a powerful prayer* because it re-presents the gospels.

An Invitation

If you have never attempted emphasizing each word of the Rosary in turn, give it a try. Continue until you have emphasized them all.

> *Hail* Mary, full of grace, the Lord is with thee. Blessed art thou among women, and blessed is the fruit of thy womb, Jesus. Holy Mary, Mother of God, pray for us sinners, now and at the hour of our death. Amen.
> Hail *Mary*, full of grace . . .
> Hail Mary, *full* of grace . . .
> Hail Mary, full of *grace* . . .
> Hail Mary, full of grace, the *Lord* is with thee . . .

Ask the Lord to reveal to you—or remind you in a fresh way—of the living, breathing reality of the Gospel that is contained in this ancient prayer.

God Prompt–LOVE the Word

I chose the narrative for this LOVE the Word exercise because Mary Magdalene provides a lovely example of Mary's gift of lowliness through her own veil and hair.

L | Listen

> Six days before the Passover, Jesus came to Bethany, where Lazarus was, whom Jesus had raised from the dead. There they made him a supper; Martha served, and Lazarus was one of those at

table with him. Mary took a pound of costly ointment of pure nard and anointed the feet of Jesus
and wiped his feet with her hair; and the house
was filled with the fragrance of the ointment.

But Judas Iscariot, one of his disciples (he
who was to betray him), said, "Why was this ointment not sold for three hundred denarii and given
to the poor?" This he said, not that he cared for
the poor but because he was a thief, and as he had
the money box he used to take what was put into
it. Jesus said, "Let her alone, let her keep it for the
day of my burial. The poor you always have with
you, but you do not always have me." (Jn 12:1–8)

O | *Observe*

Place yourself in this narrative, first as Jesus, then as Mary
Magdalene, and, lastly, as Judas. What do you see, hear,
smell, taste, and feel on or against your skin? What are
your thoughts and emotions from each point of view as
the episode plays out?

V | *Verbalize*

Talk to God about whatever rises up in your heart and
mind. What do you sense he might want you to do this
week? How do you feel about that?

E | *Entrust*

Perhaps you'd like to take a few minutes to sit at Jesus'
feet, like Mary Magdalene.

4

$\mathcal{H}$e ... Has Done Great Things for Me

(Luke 1:49)

Confessing His Blessings Upon Your Life

Whenever I think of "the lowly" referenced in Mary's Magnificat, I often think of those whose poverty and lack of educational opportunities have ensnared families from one generation to the next. One example that comes to mind is Fantasia Barrino, the 2004 *American Idol* winner who faked out the entire staff of the show and the whole country by pretending to be able to read well. She later confided in a *20/20* interview that she had signed record deals and contracts with legalese she could neither read nor understand.

Whether due to a learning disability, issues with her school system, or something else entirely, having dropped out of school in ninth grade following a sexual assault, Fantasia was functionally illiterate. While competing on the show, she performed only songs she already knew;

when this became impossible, she would listen to the words over and over until she learned them. When she had to read scripted text, she tried sounding out difficult words on the teleprompter, and when the production staff corrected inevitable errors, she memorized how to say the text correctly. She went on to win the competition with none the wiser and later sought help learning to read and write more proficiently.

I am sure it was humbling for Fantasia to admit her struggles with literacy to the world, but I confess being humbled *by* her story. What daring. What risk. What a remarkable testimony to the human desire to dream big, to do and achieve "great things." Fantasia continues to maximize her opportunities and her stunning career continues to testify of a lowly young woman's simple faith.

Contrast this to Mary's expression, "He has done great things *for me*." Mary sees in her own experience an example of the way God is. Her "great things" included becoming the Mother of God; because of this, so *many* great things were bestowed on her—and upon all of us. Hers is a truly blessed and unequalled place in the whole of mankind: namely, that she had a child by the Father in heaven, "and such a Child."

In his work "On the Magnificat," Martin Luther declared:

> She herself is unable to find a name for this work, it is too exceeding great; all she can do is break out in the fervent cry, they are "great things," impossible to describe or define. Hence men have crowded all her glory into a single word, calling her the Mother of God. No one can say anything greater of her or to her, though he had as many tongues as there are leaves on the trees, or grass in the fields, or stars in the

sky, or sand by the sea. It needs to be pondered
in the heart, what it means to be the Mother of
God.[1]

Once, Mary learned from the song of Hannah and all
the Old Testament that God brings down the proud but
blesses the lowly who look to him for mercy. But now she
has found it to be true in her own experience. Probably it
is because she had learned it so well from scripture that
she was ready and able to experience it herself. And not
just for herself but for everyone.

He Has Done Great Things for Me

For a long time I had been dealing with itchy skin that
began at the base of my neck at the hairline, then also
appeared in an area around my lower stomach and finally
developed on my chest. I knew it was psychosomatic
because it always got worse when I was stressed; I would
literally claw myself until I bled.

It seemed the itchiness always flared up when I was
about to embark on something new in ministry. I was con-
fused about what to do about this. I did not know at the
time that our bodies experience good and bad stress the
same way. Because I believed these exciting opportunities
were from God, I assumed that my stress was a kind of
good stress. I figured I was just excited (and still am) to
be doing everything God was inviting me to try. Yes, I felt
the pressure of demands and deadlines, but my dreams
were coming true to a degree I never imagined possible.
I was having the time of my life. Really. However, my
anxiety and stress were clearly taking a toll on my body
at a level that was disproportionate to the excitement and
the growth of my ministry.

Unsure of what to do, I tried to find the answer in the Bible. The readings in my LOVE the Word practice seemed to affirm my call and goals but didn't answer my problem specifically. My doctor treated the physical symptoms, but I knew in my heart that there was a deeper root that still needed to be resolved. I just didn't know how.

I talked to God about it repeatedly. *Why was I experiencing such an acute physical reaction? What was I not in touch with in myself?* I prayed: *Is this stress good stress? I am busy, but not too busy. I keep my Sundays through rest and worship, just as you taught me. I practice self-care and am otherwise physically healthy. I feel as though my other responsibilities are in balance: The kids are well adjusted and emotionally rooted. My marriage is healthy. What is* wrong *with me?*

Just as the itchiness grew intolerable, I happened to read about the use of art therapy in medicine to reveal underlying emotional and spiritual issues that can cause and exacerbate physical illness. Intrigued, I tried the exercise in the book and was absolutely blown away at what I learned was causing my itchiness.[2] It turns out I was conflicted.

While it is true that I felt excited about the growth in my ministry, I also had a nagging, unconscious belief that in the spiritual realm, reaching for goals is proud and ambitious, lacking humility, even though in the secular world, setting and attaining goals is healthy and admirable. See the hidden, underlying conflict? Reaching is bad; reaching is good. The more goals I set and reached, the more itchy I became!

In addition to this conflict, I spent the first two-thirds of my life working with God through emotional wounds stemming from my relationship with my father (as I shared at length in my first book, *Unleashed*). Throughout my formation, God has used circumstances in which I attempted goals out of obedience but failed painfully to heal me of that wound. He wanted me to experience his unconditional love and to learn to be totally dependent upon him. Logically, I saw how God had used my reaching-then-failing episodes to heal me of a deep wound (good). But emotionally, failing was painful (bad), and as a child, pain always meant I was being punished for being wrong or bad. Hence the second conflict regarding reaching.

In time, I was able to find peace and resolve this deep wound from my childhood. He has done great things for *me*. And now, when I experience the itch, I understand and know how to transform the way my spirit and body experience ministry deadlines and pressures. And as I find constructive outlets for the stress—in particular, exercise, waiting on God's provision, and confessing my trust in him—these physical manifestations of stress are greatly diminished.

Sometimes when I find myself fussing and fretting over the circumstances of my life, I wonder how Mary managed the pressures in her life. Because she continually relinquished control of her life to God, as his handmaiden, she was able to remain at the same time strong and submissive. Her Magnificat seems to make it clear she did not reach for being the mother of the Messiah or anything else at all. But I bet she reached to be the very best mother she could possibly be once she understood her role.

What a tremendous model she is for each of us. As we grow in our understanding of the role God has for us, each of us (like her) can truly say, "He has done great things for me."

A Beautiful Paradox: Greatness in Our Diversity

Each of us bears a certain lowliness that God desires to use as the raw material for great things. In many cases, we are carrying a kind of woundedness and lack of self-worth that makes us doubt that God wants to do something wonderful with our lives, but that can be a basis for a great work of God.

As I've seen him work in my heart and build the ministry he has entrusted to me, I've seen him accomplish many great things—some of which I've been dreaming of since childhood. I certainly do not deserve such grace and can never earn it. And yet his gifts are plenteous and the grace is there.

This is true for each of us, if we are willing to make ourselves lowly and allow God to exalt us to the place he wants us to be. Because we all are lowly in one way or another, the variations of "great things" that God can do in each of us is splendidly varied. But few of us lean into our lowliness enough, the way Mary did, to ask God to use it however he might desire to. The saints, too, embody this unique sense of Magnificat; as we study them, we begin to realize that we can all say together with Mary that "he has done great things for me."

Consider for a moment the great diversity that we see among the saints: St. Paul the Jewish Pharisee and St. Luke the Gentile. Peter the sanguine and John the intuitive. The soaring intellect of Thomas Aquinas alongside the learning challenges of the Curé of Ars. The largesse of Augustine compared to the hiddenness Thérèse of Lisieux. Francis's love of animals and John of the Cross's affinity for poetry. Dorothy Day's social justice crusade and Maximillian Kolbe's single act of personal substitution. The darkness of Teresa of Calcutta beside the illumination of John Paul II.

Our differentness is purposeful. Differences and limitations are not meant to be excuses for conflict or mediocrity but the occasion for a unique work of God's power. What am I most afraid of? Where are my greatest limitations? What might God do with my own lowliness if I entrust it to him?

The Almighty condescends to Mary's lowliness and does a great thing for her: he makes her the Virgin Mother of God. It is such a singular and unimaginable miracle that forevermore heaven and earth will acknowledge Mary's blessedness. St. Thomas Aquinas maintained that the Incarnation of the Word is a greater work than the creation of the whole world.[3]

Announced to the angels from the foundation of the world and to humanity at the Protoevangelium, this exceptional plan and work prepares and effects all of Mary's beatitude: she is the Immaculate Conception, sinless one, "full of grace," Mother of God, Ever-Virgin, the New Eve, the Assumption, Mother and Sign of the Church, and Queen of Heaven. Mary is the full complement of the Trinity, because the Holy Spirit came to her, the Father overshadowed her, and the Son dwelt within her.[4]

And Holy Is His Name

In one of my favorite stanzas of Handel's *Messiah*, we find the prophecy from Isaiah that "his name will be called *Wonderful* Counselor, Mighty God, Everlasting Father, Prince of Peace" (Is 9:6, emphasis added). Hebrew proper names have a definite significance in telling who and what a person or thing is, rather than simply what it or he is called.

Judges 13 tells us about another barren woman and her husband, Manoah. The angel of the Lord appeared to her and announced that she would conceive and bear a son. His name would be Samson, and he would be a consecrated Nazarite from birth. The angel instructed her to observe the Nazarite vow, herself, in preparation for Samson who would deliver God's people from the oppression of their enemies.

Manoah asked the man what his name was so that when his wife gave birth they could credit him with the prophecy. The angel of the Lord said, "Why do you ask my name, seeing it is wonderful?" (Jgs 13:18). One version renders it, "Why do you ask my name, seeing is *too* wonderful?" Another translation says the name is "mysterious"; still another that it is "secret."

In this case, the secret is the name of the angel of the Lord, and it is secret because it is too wonderful. Wow. Like the weight of the presence of the Lord is too unbearably glorious for the natural eye to alight upon.

Too wonderful.

Can the smell of rain be too wet? Are a baby's toes too fat? Is spring too fresh, ice cream too cold, grace too amazing? Is a symphony too soaring, football too competitive, or a bass too big? The ocean too noble? What name could be so wonderful that it must be secret?

Contrast "too wonderful" with how, in a display of tender condescension and an invitation to intimacy with him, the existence behind all existence, the consciousness behind all consciousness, revealed his unspeakable name to humanity through Moses.

> In revealing his mysterious name, YHWH ("I
> AM HE WHO IS," "I AM WHO AM" or "I AM
> WHO I AM"), God says who he is and by what
> name he is to be called. This divine name is
> mysterious just as God is mystery. It is at once
> a name revealed and something like the refusal
> of a name, and hence it better expresses God as
> what he is—infinitely above everything that we
> can understand or say: he is the "hidden God,"
> his name is ineffable, and he is the God who
> makes himself close to men. (CCC 206)

Add to it that he revealed his glory to Moses in the
cleft of the rock by announcing his name in a divine lit-
any of thirty-five terms. All of this communicates that
God desires to be known and loved despite his being too
wonderful to be borne.

So how could Mary bear him?

Only in her absolute purity, a unique and special gift
to her. Like Manoah's wife, Mary's vow of consecration
would be the womb for the deliverer—first her, then him.
Glorious. Marvelous. Matchless.

Mary says that the Almighty has done great things
for her, and "holy is his name." The designation of God
as almighty, that is, *powerful or capable, able,* is used as a
proper name, Almighty, throughout the scriptures. It is
the same term from which the angel Gabriel's name is
derived, that is, the strength ("power" in Greek) of God.

"The name of the LORD is a strong tower," a safe
place, says Proverbs 18:10, as though beckoning us to
test the name. There is strength in the name of the Lord.
There is power in the name of the Lord. There is hope in
the name of the Lord.

What does this mean? Not to know is vanity, possibly a mortal sin, even: "You shall not take the name of

the LORD your God in vain: for the LORD will not hold him guiltless who takes his name in vain" (Dt 5:11).

The third commandment, "You shall not take the name of the LORD your God in vain," is most often applied to cursing or similar abuse of his name, but in the scriptures "vanity" is consistently used to illustrate worthlessness, emptiness, or futility (see Ecclesiastes). Therefore, rather than something we necessarily do, it is more often something we don't do.

When we neglect to call on the name of the Lord, we have taken his name in vain; his name lies empty for us. We do not know it or experience it, and so we render it worthless in our lives. This is the fullness of what it means to "take the name of the Lord your God in vain." The name of the Lord is salvation, so that Jesus can promise, "whatever you ask in my name, I will do it" (Jn 14:13).

When the Lord said to pray in his name and he would do whatever we asked, he did not mean we should tag "in Jesus' name" or "in the name of the Father, the Son, and the Holy Spirit" to the closing of each prayer. To pray in Jesus' name is to pray according to the body of his teachings.

Ancient rabbis were accustomed to teaching in the name of rabbinical tradition and would often ask one another in whose rabbinical name one had learned as well as taught. When Jesus taught "in the name of the Lord," he was claiming not only that his authority to teach came directly from God but also that he was uniquely qualified to instruct others about the Father's character, reputation, personality, ways, and will for men. Jesus means we should ask *according to who he is.* How do I call on the name of the Lord?

The Name above All Names

Throughout the scriptures, when God's people had unique experiences of his power, they would "name" him or the place of their experience after him. In the Genesis 16 account of Sarah and Hagar, for instance, Hagar names both the Lord and the place she encountered him. Remember that Sarah's barrenness foreshadowed Mary's "barrenness" through virginity, making Mary a type of new Sarah, according to St. Paul.

The story unfolds like this. God called Abraham and promised him a son, but to that point, Abraham's wife, Sarah, had been barren. Rather than offering her barrenness to God in simplicity, Sarah gave her maidservant, Hagar, to Abraham to conceive a child in an effort to force the promise God had given Abraham of a son. Hagar did conceive, and her child became a source of jealous conflict between the two women that continues today through their corresponding ancestors. Sarah dealt so harshly with Hagar after that that she ran away.

But God found Hagar by a stream in the desert and gave her some promises of her own and afterward sent her back to submit to Sarah. She named him "The God Who Sees" (Gn 16:13) and the place of her encounter by the stream was named Beerlahairoi, meaning "the well of my Seer." The location is said to be between Kadesh and Bered, or "sanctuary" and "hail."

Unlike Sarah, Mary did offer the lowliness of her "barrenness"—her consecrated virginity—to God, as Manoah's wife offered her consecration as a womb for a deliverer. We know Mary did so because of the magnificence of the work he did through it.

More magnificent than conceiving a child in a barren or even consecrated womb that has marital relations is to conceive a child from a permanent virgin. Such "great things" move Mary to name him holy: "He has done great things for me, and holy is his name." Indeed. "Therefore God also has highly exalted him and bestowed on him the name which is above every name, that at the name of Jesus every knee should bow, in heaven and on earth and under the earth" (Phil 2:9–10).

Let's Review

- *God always does "great things" for us when we offer our lowliness* and woundedness to him in faith.
- *Woundedness and lowliness can have physical manifestations.* When we surrender our will to God, he can heal us spiritually, emotionally, and even physically.
- *If we humble ourselves, God exalts us* (Mt 23:12). That exaltation will entail something very different from one person to the next.
- *The name of the Lord is a strong tower* (Prv 18:10). His name is a source of strength to all those who call upon him.
- When we ask according to his teachings, "in my name," Jesus promises, *"I will do it"* (Jn 14:13–14, emphasis added).
- Conversely, *when we neglect to call on the name of the Lord* when we need help (salvation), we take his name in vain in a way; *his name lies empty for us.*
- Mary shows me that *when I call upon the name of the Lord in every circumstance, he does great things for me.*

An Invitation

After learning this principle and what it means to call on the name of the Lord, I had what I call a "pop quiz," an occasion to try it. My husband had changed jobs, and I discovered I was pregnant three months into the nine-month maternity waiting period required for a change in health insurance. Because my first delivery had been a C-section, my doctor planned that the second delivery would necessarily be the same.

Remembering that just the co-pay on the first delivery had been barely affordable, I called on the name Jehovah Jireh, The-Lord-Will-Provide, from Genesis 22, where the Lord provided a ram in the thicket as a sacrifice for Abraham in place of Isaac. I begged God to provide for us and waited with anxiety for the bill, frequently reminding him of the promise in his Word that "he who calls on the name of the Lord will be saved." Certainly, I pointed out, we needed saving!

In the end, my second delivery occurred too quickly for a C-section to take place, and the hospital eventually forgave and wrote off the bill due to dire financial circumstances that occurred later. Afterward I named him The-Lord-My-Insurance.

Where do you need to experience the name of the Lord? Let us pray.

God Prompt–LOVE the Word

L | Listen

> Remembering that the revelation of God's name was an act of intimacy inviting humanity—you— to a deeper relationship with him, take a look at

your current relationships and circumstances. Is there an occasion in which God is inviting you to call on his name and experience him more deeply?

Which of the attributes of God listed above do you need to experience right now? You can be saved in this circumstance, for "everyone who calls upon the name of the Lord will be saved." (Rom 10:13)

O | Observe

Here is a short list of some of the names God's people gave him throughout the scriptures.

Jehovah-Nissi (Ex 17:15) The-Lord-My-Banner (flag)
Jehovah-Raah (Ps 23:1) The-Lord-My-Shepherd
Jehovah-Jireh (Gn 22:14) The-Lord-Will-Provide
Jehovah-Rapha (Ex 15:26) The-Lord-That-Healeth
Jehovah-Shalom (Jgs 6:24) The-Lord-Is-Peace
Jehovah-Shamma (Ez 48:35) The-Lord-Is-There
Jehovah-Sabaoth (1 Sm 1:3) The-Lord-of-Hosts (armies)
Jehovah-Tsidkenu (Jer 23:6) The-Lord-Our-Righteousness
Jehovah-Oz (Is 12:2) The-Lord-Is-My-Strength
Jehovah-Mekoddishkem (Lv 20:8) The-Lord-Who-Sanctifies-You
Jehovah-Baal (Is 54:5) The-Lord-Your-Husband
Jehovah-Zimrath (Ex 15:2) The-Lord-My-Song
Jehovah-Nasa (Ps 99:8) The-Lord-Who-Forgives
El Roi (Gn 16:13) The-God-Who-Sees

V | Verbalize

Pause for a moment and ask God to reveal his name in your circumstance, and then wait expectantly to see how he will work. The answer may take a while, but wait for the answer even though it may tarry (see Habakkuk 2:3). Consider recording the date and answer to your prayer in the margins of these pages, or in a prayer journal. I produce an annual LOVE the Word with Mary journal expressly for this purpose.[5] Maybe you want to remind him of the promise in his name. What do you want to say to him now?

E | Entrust

Perhaps you'd like to take a few minutes to simply wonder in this extraordinary promise and entrust yourself to him anew.

5

*H*is Mercy Is on Those Who Fear Him

(Luke 1:50)

Daring to Approach God's Mercy Seat

When my sister was little, she ran to my mother after a nightmare. Attempting to soothe her fears, my mother told her she should pray to Jesus and remember he is always with her. With worry wrinkling her forehead, my sister replied, "But, Mama, I need somebody with skin on 'em!"

The tabernacle and ark of the covenant were Old Testament expressions of God's desire to be present with his people. Jesus, our new covenant, and Mary, the new ark of that covenant, carry this expression forward into the Church, where God is still present on his throne. Together, they are mercy "with skin on 'em."

As Pope Francis encourages us, "Let us be renewed by God's mercy, let us be loved by Jesus, let us enable the power of his love to transform our lives too; and let us become agents of this mercy."[1]

In order to become agents of mercy, however, we must first experience that mercy for ourselves. We must dare to approach the mercy seat and acknowledge our need for that merciful presence to bring healing and relief to our broken places . . . and to glorify and praise the One who came to earth that we might be redeemed and our relationship with God restored. This work of redemption was uniquely foreshadowed in the exodus, where God directed his Chosen People to build the tabernacle as well as the sign of his presence among them: the ark of the covenant.

A Closer Look at the Ark of the Covenant

In the Old Testament, the seat of God's mercy was the ark of the covenant. Located in the holy of holies, the innermost chamber of the tabernacle, the ark was the most important object inside. Measuring only about three feet by one and a half feet, it was partitioned off on one side by a richly woven veil in blue, scarlet, and purple thread with ornate cherubim embroidered in gold; it was enclosed on the three remaining sides with wood paneling overlaid with gold.

The ark rested inside the holy of holies, protected and revered, a visible symbol of the Lord's presence among them. Inside the small box were three articles of great religious significance: the tablets of Moses containing the ten words (the Ten Commandments), a golden urn of manna, and Aaron's fruited almond staff. All were fitting reminders of God's perpetual provision for his beloved people.

The lid of the ark was decorated with two of the glorious, worshipping cherubim, beaten from one piece of gold that further enclosed the lid of the ark within the covering of their wings. In this way, the ark was carefully surrounded by worship, privacy, and mystery.

The lid of the ark was called the *mercy seat*. Once a year, on the great Day of Atonement, the high priest entered the holy of holies to sprinkle the sacrificial blood of atonement there (see Leviticus 16). The Day of Atonement was the highest holy day of the Israelite year, the only day anyone was allowed inside the holy of holies, and even then it could only be the high priest (v. 2). The high priest sprinkled the blood of atonement on the mercy seat seven times on this day, for his own sins and those of the whole people of God. For that reason, the term *mercy seat* is sometimes used interchangeably with *propitiation* or *expiation* (see Hebrews 9:5, NABRE), meaning "appeasement or satisfaction of wrath."

The seat of the ark was both a throne and oracle for God as well as a sign that was later fulfilled in the person of Jesus. And just as the mercy seat represented expiation in the Old Testament, so Christ fulfilled that role under the new covenant. St. John points out, "In this is love: not that we have loved God, but that he loved us and sent his Son as *expiation* for our sins" (1 Jn 4:10, NABRE, emphasis added).

St. Paul elaborates: "They are justified by his grace as a gift, through the redemption which is in Christ Jesus, whom God put forward as an *expiation* by his blood, to be received by faith. This was to show God's righteousness, because in his divine forbearance he had passed over former sins; it was to prove at the present time that he himself is righteous and that he justifies him who has faith in Jesus" (Rom 3:24–26, emphasis added).

Jesus is more than just the atoning sacrifice, however. He is also the high priest: "He had to be made like his brethren in every respect, so that he might become a merciful and faithful high priest in the service of God, to make *expiation* for the sins of the people" (Heb 2:17, emphasis added). The Douay-Rheims translation puts the second part of that verse in a slightly different way: "That he might be a *propitiation* for the sins of the people."

God's mercy was shown to us not merely with feelings of sympathy (he did not merely feel sorry for us) but with action. He bent toward us in a glorious divine paradox, sending Jesus as both priest and victim. Mercy and justice, grace and propitiation, have "kissed" (Ps 85:10), so that St. James can say, "Mercy triumphs over judgment" (Jas 2:13). Mercy is God's noblest and most enduring work; the face of God's justice and mercy are offered to us in the face of Jesus.

His Name Is Mercy

As we explored in the last chapter, all Hebrew names, especially personal names, were supposed to bear a certain significance and therefore were carefully and solemnly selected. So connected were an individual and his name that the latter was frequently used as an equivalent of the former: "to be called" meant "to be"; the name was understood to be identical with the person or thing.

Nothing testifies more eloquently to this fact than the religious awe in which the Hebrews held God's name, I AM WHO AM, revealed to Moses from the burning bush. When God sheltered Moses in the cleft of the rock in order to offer him a further experience of his glory, it is interesting to me that God's act of tender condescension is said to be a work of his mercy: "And he said, 'I will make all my goodness pass before you, and will proclaim before you my name "The LORD"; and I will be gracious to whom

I will be gracious, and will show mercy on whom I will show mercy'" (Ex 33:19).

That God uttered his name to Moses as he passed by is striking to me, particularly because it is not the ineffable name he had *already* revealed from the bush. Instead, it seems to be an elaboration or explanation of sorts:

> And the LORD descended in the cloud and stood with him there, and proclaimed the name of the LORD. The LORD passed before him, and proclaimed, "The LORD, the LORD, a God *merciful* and gracious, slow to anger, and abounding in steadfast love and faithfulness, *keeping steadfast love for thousands*, forgiving iniquity and transgression and sin, but who will by no means clear the guilty, visiting the iniquity of the fathers upon the children and the children's children, to the third and the fourth generation." (Ex 34:5–7, emphasis added)

As the Lord moved by Moses, he spoke his name using these fifty-eight words. Imagine him swooping from the edge of the universe to settle in the space beside you right now. What would his presence feel like? A slight breeze? A hurricane? Stifling? Hot? Tingly?

From inside the unearthly cloud, the expressive voice interpreted himself, unforgettably establishing the foundation of our understanding him. The scriptures say his voice sounds like many waters, rolling thunder, and the noise of an army. Certainly, there remain parts of God's limitless, eternal character that are too rich for the human mind to grasp. Yet his radical desire for our knowledge of him necessitated his explaining himself to us in a small, understandable way. How thoughtful and accommodating our God must be.

Moses's experience of God's glory that day must have been a wondrous mystery. It calls to mind the old hymn:

> A wonderful Savior is Jesus my Lord, a won-
> derful Savior to me,
> He hideth my soul in the cleft of the rock,
> where rivers of rapture I see.
> He hideth my soul in the cleft of the rock that
> shadows a dry thirsty land;
> He hideth my life in the depths of His love,
> and covers me there with His hand,
> And covers me there with His hand.[2]

Look back at the passage in Exodus 34:5–7, where God hid Moses in the cleft of the rock. Did you notice mercy in his name? The phrase "keeping steadfast love" is sometimes translated "keeping mercy." How does he keep mercy? By revealing his name. By allowing us to see something of his glory. By taking away iniquity, wickedness, and sin. By judging guilt justly. Yet even his justice is tempered with mercy that reaches to the third and fourth generations.

Mother of Mercy, Ark of the New Covenant

What is this mercy? The word *Savior* (or *salvation*) denotes God's mercy. Jesus is our mercy seat, the place where God's justice and mercy intersect: "There is therefore now no condemnation for those who are in Christ Jesus" (Rom 8:1).

Mary is the mother of mercy because Jesus is the face of God's mercy. In the Magnificat she exclaims that "his mercy is on those who fear him" (Lk 1:50). Nowhere is this covering presence more clearly seen than in Mary, who, like the seat of the Old Testament tabernacle ark, was overshadowed by the presence of God and conceived. We see this hovering, life-giving presence at work several places in scripture:

- *At creation:* Genesis 1:2 depicts the spirit of God "*moving* over the face of the waters " (emphasis added).
- *In the exodus, where God's visible presence took the form of a cloud by day and pillar of fire by night:* "And Moses was not able to enter the tent of meeting, because the cloud *abode* upon it, and the glory of the LORD filled the tabernacle" (Ex 40:35, emphasis added).
- *At the annunciation:* "And the angel said to her, "The Holy Spirit will come upon you, and the power of the Most High will *overshadow* you" (Lk 1:35, emphasis added; it is interesting to note that the same Greek word, *episkiazōs,* is used in both the Exodus and Luke passages).

Mary's unique role as the new ark is hinted at by St. Luke in his description of the annunciation. He places in Elizabeth's mouth nearly the same words (though with a far more joyful context) that David speaks while bringing the ark up to Jerusalem in 2 Samuel 6: "How can the ark of the LORD come to me?" (v. 9).

In the Hebrews passage about the old and new covenants (chapters 8–9), Jesus is depicted as the high priest: "But when Christ appeared as a high priest of the good things that have come, then through the greater and more perfect tent (not made with hands, that is, not of this creation) he entered once for all into the Holy Place, taking not the blood of goats and calves but his own blood, thus securing an eternal redemption" (Heb 9:11–12).

Earlier in this same passage, we find the ark "entirely covered with gold" and containing the manna, the staff, and the tablets of the covenant.

Each of these elements referenced in this passage point to Jesus, the fulfillment of the covenant promises, whom Mary carried in her womb:

- The "tablets of stone" of the old covenant anticipated the "Word became flesh" in the new (Jn 1:14).
- The resurrected stick of Aaron's authority foreshadowed the one whose Resurrection would conquer death itself (see John 11:25; 1 Peter 1:3).
- The golden urn of manna that sustained the Chosen People for forty years in the desert found perfect fulfillment in Jesus, the Bread of Life (see John 6:52–58).

In the book of Revelation, the apostle John makes a reference to the ark—which at that time had been lost for six centuries—that would have shocked any first-century Jew: "Then God's temple in heaven was opened, and *the ark of his covenant was seen within his temple.* . . . And a great portent appeared in heaven, a woman clothed with the sun, with the moon under her feet, and on her head a crown of twelve stars; she was with child" (Rv 11:19, 12:1–2, emphasis added).

When the heavenly temple is opened, the lost ark is seen as the woman "clothed with the sun" who bore the child. This is none other than Mary—the ark of the new covenant—who bore Jesus, the new covenant. For all these reasons and more, the Church Fathers understood and wrote of Mary this way as early as the second century:

> At that time, the Savior coming from the Virgin, the Ark, brought forth His own Body into the

world from that Ark, which was gilded with pure gold within by the Word, and without by the Holy Ghost; so that the truth was shown forth, and the Ark was manifested. . . . And the Savior came into the world bearing the incorruptible Ark, that is to say His own body.[3]

Another example, this one from the third century, is from Gregory Thaumaturgus, who intones, "Let us chant the melody which has been taught us by the inspired harp of David, and say, 'Arise, O Lord, into Thy rest; Thou, and the ark of Thy sanctuary.' For the holy Virgin is in truth an ark, wrought with gold both within and without, that has received the whole treasury of the sanctuary."[4]

What about Mary?

As I look back on that time in my life, I find it impossible to overstate my bafflement regarding the Church's teachings on Mary when I was researching my way into the Catholic Church. Frankly, right up to the time of my confirmation I was scandalized by the incredible claims the Church makes about her. Even after I joined the Church, I was disturbed by the assertions that God predestined, created, and preserved Mary in lifelong sinlessness and ever-virginity.

Why would God do such a thing? It seemed irrational, in my mind, to justify God *desiring* to elevate anyone but Christ—who is divine and therefore "worthy"—to such privilege. And yet I had read the Fathers in their own words. I knew the Catholic Church is the only church to sustain and defend these teachings from the time of the apostles. This huge gap in theology is partly why cleaving to tradition *and* scripture is so necessary. The historical Church explains,

> The Holy Fathers, we say, are of supreme authority, whenever they all interpret in one and the same manner any text of the Bible, as pertaining to the doctrine of faith or morals; for their unanimity clearly evinces that such interpretation has come down from the Apostles as a matter of Catholic faith." (*Providentissimus Deus* 14)

And also, "We receive those doctrines which they thus teach, not merely because they teach them, but because they bear witness that all Christians everywhere then held them."[5]

That being the case, the one question that remains to be resolved in the minds of most thoughtful believers regarding the Church's claims regarding Mary is the simple question *why*. What possible reason could God have for preserving Mary as both the perpetual ark of the new covenant and as the sinless, ever-virgin New Eve—as Church history and our Christian heritage say God did?

The answer is eschatological and lies in Jesus, from the beginning of salvation history all the way to his Second Coming and the marriage feast that will consummate the new heavens and new earth.

From Generation to Generation

Perhaps because Americans have no history before 1776, a mere two hundred–plus years, we have little patience for millennia or slow evolution "from generation to generation." We want it all; and we want it all *right now*.

My former-Protestant understanding of Israel's promise and fulfillment of the Messiah was typically shortsighted in this way. We placed our Nativity sets out at Christmas, maybe read the Christmas story from the Bible, and stopped all consideration of Mary there. And we had precedent for such a short view: every Israelite alive expected a merely human Messiah with a typical political system, and every married woman in Israel hoped to be the Messiah's mother in the normal way. How else could it be?

But why should we assume Mary's promises stop there if Abraham's promises, Moses's promises, David's promises, Paul's promises—*all* of these promises—extend far beyond their own lifetimes and the first fulfillments that these particular people experienced into "end times" terms? How could this long view not also be true of Mary as well?

Not only is she "blessed among women," according to scripture, but even through the miracle of her conceiving and giving birth to Jesus despite her consecrated celibacy, she is "full of grace"—sinless—by a special work of her Savior (Lk 1:28, 47). She is "overshadowed" like the first ark (see Exodus 40:35, Luke 1:35). She is betrothed, but resolved to remain a consecrated virgin: "How can this be . . . ?" (Lk 1:34).

This ever-virgin woman is the fulfillment of the promise in Genesis 3 and the "great sign" of Revelation 12. She is mother by direct action from God himself with no human intervention, an unimagined, unforeseen possibility up to this point in Israelite and human history. This new, divine motherhood embraces all of those "who keep the commandments of God and bear testimony to Jesus," her Son (Rv 12:17).

From the moment of his miraculous Incarnation within her, God began directing messianic kingdom expectations to a new Israel and its ultimate spiritual finality in the Church—a New Eve for his New Adam, a new ark for his new covenant, a spotless bride for his bridegroom—that will continue until history ends and is fulfilled at the Second Coming.

Jesus affirmed this eschatological long view by directing our own expectations further ahead than human mother- and fatherhood through his teachings on the absolute indissolubility of marriage and the even higher state of celibacy. He was celibate, as was his mother. Together they are the New Adam and the New Eve, and both point us far beyond themselves.

> Virginity for the sake of the kingdom of heaven is . . . a powerful sign of the supremacy of the bond with Christ and of the ardent expectation of his return, a sign which also recalls that marriage is a reality of this present age which is passing away. . . . Esteem of virginity for the sake of the kingdom and the Christian understanding of marriage are inseparable, and they reinforce each other. (CCC 1619–1620)

With the most splendid consistency from generation to generation, the New Adam and New Eve; the new ark and the new covenant; the bridegroom and bride—pure and virgin, celibate but fecund—give *spiritual* birth to a kingdom of *spiritual* children through the Holy Spirit. This kingdom will, for its perfection and divine genesis, endure throughout the generations for all eternity.

"As St. Irenaeus says, 'Being obedient she became the cause of salvation for herself and for the whole human race.' Hence not a few of the early Fathers gladly assert . . . : 'The

knot of Eve's disobedience was untied by Mary's obedience: what the virgin Eve bound through her disbelief,
Mary loosened by her faith'" (CCC 494). Comparing her
with Eve, they call Mary "the Mother of the living" and
frequently claim: "Death through Eve, life through Mary."

Thy Kingdom Come

We are the Body of Christ, and Christ was born of Mary.
Precisely because the kingdom to come is to be fulfilled
in flesh and blood, its beginning is in the mother. Mary's
motherhood is the sign of our new covenant with God,
who is himself pure spirit. Her perpetually sinless, virgin motherhood is the beginning and prototype of the
Church, the spotless Bride of Christ, every sin forgiven
and purified by his sacrifice.

Some Christians experience great difficulty in
accepting the truth about Mary in part because they have
rejected Jesus and Paul the teachings on celibacy, and, to a
great degree, they have refused to adhere to the teachings
of scripture concerning the indissolubility of marriage.
(Marriage is permanent because it is a sign of the permanent bond between Christ and his Church, according to
Paul in Ephesians 5:22–33). Conversely, understanding
Mary's spiritual motherhood, flowing from both her virginity and her maternity by God's design, is the transfor-
mative sign that challenges me to live out the Church's
teachings—even those I find hard to understand—with
greater faith and obedience.

Mary remains both sinless and virgin, because, like
the Church she signifies, her motherhood is completely,
utterly, eternally spiritual and pure—giving birth to the
Word in innumerable spiritual children, all conceived
by the Holy Spirit and born of God. She nurtures our

holiness so that we, too, can give birth to the Word in the world as well, through faith.

As Pope John Paul II said, "Unless one looks to the Mother of God, it is impossible to understand the mystery of the Church, her reality, her essential vitality. . . . There is an analogy in God's salvific economy: if we wish to understand it fully in relation to the whole of human history, we cannot omit, in the perspective of our faith, the mystery of 'woman': virgin-mother-spouse" (*Mulieris Dignitatem* 22).

And so, "his mercy is on those who fear him from generation to generation." As God's presence dwelt on the mercy seat atop the ark of the covenant in the innermost chamber of the tabernacle in the holy of holies, Mary's specially created purity and free assent to the Father's will brought his Spirit down to overshadow and dwell in her as the new ark that would bring his mercy to us all. Mary assures me through her Magnificat that God is always extending his mercy to me in order to cleanse me of sin and exalt me through the deepest possible intimacy with him.

Let's Review

- *God's merciful love has always been with his people.* In the Old Testament, that love was expressed through God's mercy seat (the ark of the covenant); the ark was located in the holy of holies, the most intimate and sacred place on earth, where the presence of God rested on the mercy seat.
- *The Old Testament ark foreshadowed Mary*, who carried the fulfillment of the previous covenant in her womb. In the New Testament, Jesus is the embodiment of

the new covenant, and Mary is the ark of the new covenant.

- The Old Testament ark of the covenant in the tabernacle *contained the Ten Commandments, Aaron's blossoming staff, and a golden urn of manna.* All three were signs of Christ, who fulfilled the law, was raised to new life, and was the bread of life.
- *The seat of the ark was called the mercy seat* because the blood of atonement was offered there once a year for the whole people of God. The New Testament calls Jesus, whose blood atones eternally for our sins, our mercy seat (see Hebrews 9:11–13).
- *The dogmatic teachings of the Church regarding Mary,* such as her perpetual virginity and personal sinlessness, *originate from the times of the apostles.* Yet asking why inspires a journey of faith that leads us closer to both Mary and to her Son.
- St. Irenaeus: *"The knot of Eve's disobedience was untied by Mary's obedience."*
- Mary assures me through her Magnificat that *God extends his mercy to every generation.*
- *God's mercy draws me to purification and exalts me* to union with him.

Invitation

Through her Magnificat, Mary teaches me that a relationship with God through the scriptures *and* tradition draws me into the merciful intimacy with God that he wants for me. This intimacy is what makes me a kind of magnificat, able to give birth to the Word in the world in my own unique way, in my own generation, similar to the way she did. In essence, the "holy of holies" of my soul, similar to Mary's, becomes the place where God rules and reigns in me.

God Prompt–LOVE the Word

L | Listen

"And his mercy is on those who fear him from generation to generation" (Lk 1:50).

O | Observe

Sometime this week, visit someone in your family who is old. If there is no one in your family who is aged or who lives close by enough for a visit, go to a nursing home unannounced and ask permission to visit an elderly patient who rarely has visitors.

V | Verbalize

Talk to this person about God's mercy. What do you have in common? What is different?

E | Entrust

Before you leave, pray for this person and all his or her ancestors and descendants. In your prayer, entrust them all to God along with your own ancestors and descendants. Ask God to bless and help your new friend and add him or her to your daily prayer list.

6

$\mathcal{H}$e Has Shown Strength with His Arm

(Luke 1:51)

God's Power in Human Weakness

At this point in the Magnificat, we embark on the second half of Mary's hymn of praise, what we might call the second spiritual movement of the canticle (cf. Luke 1: 51–55). Mary's fiat, her yes, is the axis of salvation, past and future. So her song takes on the whole sweep of salvation history, as though the whole of God's people to that point is celebrating his slow movement of grace, and we ourselves continue to do so by looking back in the scriptures and liturgy of the Church, all of us together from generation to generation.

In the original Greek of Luke's gospel, there are seven verbs of magnificent continuing action in the Magnificat: he has *shown* strength with his arm; he has *scattered* the proud; he has *put down* the mighty; he has *exalted* those of low degree; he has *filled* the hungry; he has *sent away empty*; and he has *helped* his servant Israel.

In essence, the perpetual action of each Greek verb construction says, "God has shown strength, he is showing strength, and he will show strength." Seven is the biblical number for completeness, covenant, and divinity. Evident in these seven divine works that sweep up all of salvation history into a type of covenant synopsis is the style in which the Lord of history works: he places himself on the side of the most insignificant.

Often, God's plan is hidden when the proud, the mighty, and the rich seem to win out, over and over. But always, in the end, his strength (his name) is shown to those who are faithful to his Word: the humble, the hungry, his servant Israel, namely, the community of the People of God that, like Mary, are all poor, pure, and simple of heart.

Jesus encourages fearlessness in this "little flock," since the Father has willed to give them the kingdom (cf. Lk 12:32). Mary's Magnificat invites us to take up with this little flock, to really be part of the people of God of history in purity and simplicity of heart, in love of God, specifically by waiting on God to reveal the strength of his arm.

A few Church theologians, specifically Sts. Bede and Theophylact, understand "his arm" to mean the Son of God incarnate in the Virgin, for Jesus is the power and wisdom of God (see 1 Corinthians 1:24). Either way, the point of the phrase "the strength of his arm" is *breaking spiritual pride*.

Humble Yourself and Be Exalted

In the Bible, the "arm of God" refers to God's own power, by which he works without the help of any creature (see John 12:38, Acts 13:17). He uses the creature who humbles him- or herself to others before him, but they are completely oblivious at the time. All the action is done quietly and in secret, and nobody is aware of it until it is all accomplished; so that this power, or arm, can be known and understood at first only by faith.

In a Messianic Servant Song, Isaiah complains that too few have faith in this arm, saying, "Who has believed what we have heard? And to whom has the arm of the LORD been revealed?" (Is 53:1). These things are so because, as he goes on to say, everything is done in secret and without any appearance of power.

Something similar is indicated in Habakkuk 3:4 where horns (or "rays") protrude from God's hands as a sign of his mighty power and authority; and yet "there he veiled his power." Again in Psalm 77:15, 19–20: "Thou didst with thy arm redeem thy people. . . . Thy way was through the sea, thy path through the great waters; yet thy footprints were unseen. Thou didst lead thy people like a flock by the hand of Moses and Aaron."

This is how the godly experience the strength of his arm. God works for his people, his flock, with his own arm. A person or thing is destroyed or raised up before anyone knows it, and no one sees it done. He allows the godly to become powerless and weak—to be brought very low—until everyone supposes their end is just around the corner.

And then, in the very things that seem about to destroy them, he is present with great power yet so hidden and secret that even they who suffer the oppression feel it all while somehow still believing and hoping in him. There is the fullness of God's power and his outstretched arm. For where man's strength ends, God's strength begins, provided his faithful one calls on his name and waits on him.

St. Paul learned this principle through his suffering: "But he said to me, 'My grace is sufficient for you, for my power is made perfect in weakness.' I will all the more gladly boast about my weaknesses, that the power of Christ may rest upon me" (2 Cor 12:9). This is a powerful promise that too few of God's people experience while harassed by the hurry and demands of fear and pride within themselves and against them by others.

When the oppression comes to an end, it is revealed to all what great strength was hidden underneath the weakness. Jesus was utterly vulnerable and powerless on the Cross, and yet he performed his mightiest work there, conquering sin, death, the world, hell, the devil, and all evil.

All the martyrs were strong and conquered in union with him, as are all of us who suffer and are oppressed, so that all together we are able to say with the prophet Joel, "Let the weak say, I am strong" (Jl 3:10 KJV). God's activity happens in faith and lack of positive feeling until all is accomplished.

The ungodly experience the strength of his arm differently. For those without faith or who are even enemies of God, he withdraws his power from them and lets them puff themselves up in their own strength, allowing them to become great and mighty in promoting and praising themselves and one another. When their bubble is full-blown, everyone supposes them to have won and overcome, and they themselves feel safe and secure in having achieved all they wanted, then God pops the bubble and it's all over. We see a good example of this in the Exodus account of the fall and destruction of the Pharaoh (see Exodus 14).

As demanded by Moses, Pharaoh had released the Hebrew slaves after their God had sent a series of plagues upon his people. But no sooner had they gone then the Egyptian king changed his mind (see Exodus 14:5); calling for his army and chariots, he angrily pursued the people of God into the desert in order to overtake and reenslave them. Just when they were backed against the Red Sea, sure to be conquered, God parted the waters and the Israelites walked across on dry land. And when the Egyptians pursued them over that miraculous "highway" through the sea, the tsunami of water swept them completely away.

Our lack of faith prevents us from waiting long enough for him to act on our behalf, until we, too, can celebrate in jubilation that the mercy of God, together with all his might, is unequivocally with those who fear him. As Mary says here in her Magnificat, the arm of God with all power is always shown to be against the proud. Oh, ye of little faith! The psalmist reminds us, "Fret not yourself because of the wicked" (Ps 37:1). God will always show the strength of his arm on behalf of his people.

We grope in fear after the mercy and the arm of God, and, unable to feel them, suppose it's a lost cause and that our enemies have won, as though God's grace and mercy have forsaken us and his arm is turned against us. We do this because we do not know his works and his ways (see Hebrews 3:7–4:14), and therefore we do not know him, neither his mercy nor his arm.

His Strength Is Perfect

I experienced the strength of his arm after my conversion to Catholicism, the worst period in my adult life to date. I had secretly researched my way into full communion with the Church, to the utter confusion and disbelief of everyone who knew me. My denomination abandoned

me, which meant my dream of publishing Bible studies
was gone (or so I believed at the time). Most of my church
friends avoided me, looked sideways at me in the grocery
store, or stopped speaking to me altogether. My relationships with my husband and both sides of our family were
extremely strained and burdened by suspicion.

It was a stressful time in other aspects as well. I had
recently given birth to my second child and taken a sala-
ried job at my new parish, a job God had provided and for
which I had been preparing for years. Yet I had almost no
support from the parish staff; a beloved seminarian and
parish member had done the job together as volunteers
for years, and the pastor had passed over both of them in
order to give the job to me. At first I was elated to get the
job, but it was soon apparent that the entire community
believed I had somehow usurped the rightful position of
the seminarian and woman volunteer. I was maligned,
persecuted, and even stalked, until I was forced to take
legal action and report to my bishop.

At that time, my relationships in every area of my
life were particularly strained and difficult. My marriage
problems and postpregnancy hormones were pushing
me to the limit. After that, my oldest son had a devastat-
ing accident that left him alive but bedridden for several
months. Nursing a convalescent child and an infant, while
fighting off slander and lies and suspicion from every
direction, with no marital support, meant my entire world
was hard, cold, and lonely, and God seemed nowhere to
be found. People whispered behind our backs how my
husband should "get control of his family" before I led
us all to hell. Really.

I knew there would be no convincing anyone of
either the truth or my motives; I never even tried. I clung
to Mary's hand, leaning on her to strengthen me in some

semblance of the humility that could remain silent against the onslaught. And then the parish laid me off; at the same time, my husband's work hours were cut in half. We went from two incomes to a half of one and began eating from the parish's food pantry.

I have never been so profoundly humiliated in my life. What do you do when cutbacks, job losses, tragic accidents, stalkers, haters, marital strife, postpartum depression, and overwhelming debt (all at one time!) threaten to blow you away? You dare to let God exalt you. The one thing I knew from watching Mary's example was his promise that he *would* vindicate me if I stayed silent and waited long enough. And look at me now.

Look at *her* now.

God, the Creator, Almighty, hid Mary and continues to allow her to be hidden somewhat from humanity because he made her for *himself.* He intended and created and *longed* for a human being to be *able* to receive him in totality. He wanted someone of the human race, any of us— even one of us?—to fully receive his unitive love. Where none was possible through Eve, he made one possible for himself in Mary. He protected her and her Son's identities through her lowliness and humility.

But he *longs* to fully reveal her to all of history, to every fallen, doubting angel and creature, because he *can,* and *did,* and *does* such spectacular miracles through a little peasant girl. By those miracles, for himself, he made her Queen of Heaven and Earth.

If you haven't seen God *do* anything, perhaps it's because you haven't *risked* anything. Those who risk everything with him always see the strength of his arm.

In the train of life with God, he must and can only be known by the engine of faith; our senses and reason must be the caboose (see Matthew 5:29). This dependence on needing to see and feel results is the eye that offends us; therefore, it must be plucked out and cast away.

Waiting with Passion

Ever since my first Lent as a non-Catholic, when I awaited
being received into full communion with the Church at
Easter Vigil, I watch *The Passion of the Christ* movie every
year during the Triduum. It's rough; I have to force myself
not to get up and go to the restroom or get something to
eat. I make myself endure the whole, awful narrative (can
I use that word for something so violent?). I watch it as a
Lenten discipline, but in my heart, the whole time I just
wait for the movie to be over.

For several weeks after watching *The Passion*, I find
myself praying the Sorrowful Mysteries similar to the
way I talk myself through difficulty and suffering: *In
less than twenty-four hours, it will all be over. Let's just get
through this, Jesus. We're in the Garden. . . . Thank goodness,
it's morning; you made it; less than nine hours left. . . . Okay,
now we're carrying that awful cross. Can you make it up this
ugly hill? Just hang on Jesus, we're almost there and then only
three hours left . . .*

To me, *passion* has always been a strange word to
associate with these long hours of unspeakable torment.
Passion is commonly used to denote striving for personal
expression, and in this sense it is morbidly fascinating that
Jesus' suffering is said to be and truly was his Passion.

The Bible mostly uses the term *passion* to describe
out-of-control emotions and desires (see Galatians 5:24).
In the book of Acts we find the only biblical use of *passion*
in reference to Jesus' suffering and death: "To them he
presented himself alive after his passion" (Acts 1:3). From
this mustard seed of a verse sprang a beautiful theological
tree in the Church on passion, specifically as it relates to
redemptive suffering, through the suffering and death
of the Lord.

Passion Is Intentional

Just when I thought it was impossible to be more scandalized by the mystery of Jesus' Passion, I found myself reading W. H. Vanstone, who invites us to consider it in a largely unexplored way in his classic book *The Stature of Waiting*:

> The word "passion" does not mean . . . "pain." It means dependence, exposure, waiting, being no longer in control of one's own situation, being the object of what is done. . . . Jesus entered into the totality or extremity of passion—the situation in which there is no limit . . . to what one may receive or suffer; and at the great climax of the story, at the moment when He is handed over in the Garden, we see Him waiting, in the agony of expectancy, for whatever it is that He is to receive.[1]

At the Last Supper table, Jesus' hour for deliberate vulnerability has arrived: "And he said to them, 'I have earnestly desired to eat this passover with you before I suffer'" (Lk 22:15). He might have said, *I have passionately passioned to share this passion with you before my Passion*. In the words of St. Bede: "He first then desires to eat the typical Passover, and so to declare the mysteries of His Passion to the world."[2]

A hint of the mysterious depths of the Passion's real meaning came from Jesus when he saw that "all was now finished" (Jn 19:28). Yet wasn't there something else, something beyond Jesus' *doing* all that was necessary to complete his mission: Passion? He must finish his exodus (see Luke 9:31); he must pass over into the deliberate vulnerability of passive waiting.

His work, his doing, was finished. Only after the agony of passive vulnerability, from the Cross, did he finally say, "It is finished." His last declaration of the Passion is made in the embrace of extreme, passive vulnerability.

We Begin and End with Vulnerability

But just as striking as his last declaration is his first. Like us, Jesus was born into total helplessness. He chose this patient vulnerability; he leaned into it: "Though he was in the form of God, [he] did not count equality with God a thing to be grasped, but emptied himself, taking the form of a servant, being born in the likeness of men. And being found in human form he humbled himself and became obedient unto death, even death on a cross" (Phil 2:6–8).

Recognizing his helplessness at the end of his life, some would spit on him, beat him, and pierce him to death; some will marginalize or ignore him entirely. Not all, of course; just as at the beginning, those who saw the divine infant drew near to caress and cuddle him, at the end some would adore the Lord, washing and anointing his battered, broken, dead body with great love and tenderness.

And now, he waits in agony of expectation to know: *What will I do with him?*

What Will I Do with Him?

Most of what we consider life is bookended between two periods of inactive helplessness—birth/infancy and death. Passion as dependence straddles human life. Helplessness, then, cannot be inferior to independence.

This punctuation at both ends of my doing seems designed to teach, and even warn, me that neither the beginning nor the completion of my life depends on me. Therefore, the value of my lifespan is not solely dependent on the activity, work, or ability to contribute to society on which I place so much value.

So my passion will not necessarily be my doing. Instead, maybe I should consider it to be the period(s) where I transition, suddenly or gradually, into a more dependent phase of life. Maybe I am waiting. Maybe I am dependent because of age or illness. Maybe I believe I am useless or ineffective because I am completely dependent and can no longer "contribute" to family or society. Maybe I am unable to even care for myself.

This is passion the way Jesus teaches it: moving from activity to receptivity, temporarily or permanently. Jesus teaches us that passion seems to depend less on what we express in achieving and more in what we express in receiving.

"And what shall I say? 'Father, save me from this hour'? No, for this purpose I have come to this hour" (Jn 12:27). When I allow passion to be something that is done to me rather than what I do, Jesus' Passion transforms my waiting, helplessness, and uselessness from a teeth-gritting-count-down-till-it's-over to the currency of redemption and resurrection.

Jesus shows me, and Mary follows with her example, that human dignity is not diminished in vulnerability and helplessness but *accentuated* in those who have nothing left to offer. Passion is a striking corrective to the "just *do* it" mentality of our times. The world feels pity for weakness and even seeks to wipe it out, as in eugenics, altering fetal DNA, and aborting babies. But helplessness, embraced in unity with Christ, is the most powerful spiritual reality.

The weak in Christ are stronger than the strength of men. In waiting, in dependence, in weakness, I am not useless. This does not have to be some sad, unfortunate situation. By grace—only by grace—I can surrender to the detachment and the exposure of my real and raw weakness.

Like Jesus, I can offer a waiting love that does not try to rush back into or force the action. To Jesus I can offer my presence and gentleness and mercy. And it might be my leaning into this true passion that is the most important and necessary part of my life.

Have no anxiety. Pray for the strength of God's arm to be revealed in your circumstance. Give it to him completely and "pass over" with Jesus by laying it all in his hands; wait, and see what he will do!

He Has "Scattered" the Proud

This is a strange sentence, I think, probably because of the use of the word *scatter*. It literally means to "dissipate, rout, separate, squander, disperse, scatter (abroad), strew, or waste." God scatters the proud using the very purposes of their hearts: in their thoughts, their imaginings, their opinions, their estimation. He works their machinations to their own destruction, so that he confuses and beats them. Something similar is said in Job 5:12–13, "He frustrates the devices of the crafty, so that their hands achieve no success. He takes the wise in their own craftiness; and the schemes of the wily are brought to a quick end."

We see it over and over in the Old Testament: Pharaoh followed the Hebrews through the Red Sea and drowned there with his entire army in the same sea.

Joseph's brothers sold him in order to do away with him, yet God used that very circumstance to raise Joseph so high that his brothers would bow down to him. Haman, who planned to kill the Jews, was hanged with his own noose. Each of them, like each of us, is punished through his own sin (see Wisdom 11:16). What is more, sin's punishment takes the same form as the sin itself, so that "he has put down the mighty from their thrones, and exalted those of low degree" (Lk 1:52).

The proud exalt themselves, especially above those who follow God. They put down and shame the opinions and rights of believers and persecute them so that their own cause will by any and all means be right and maintained. He scatters those who are wise and prudent in their own thoughts and imaginations because they depend entirely on themselves, often at the expense of those who love and follow God. They vent their pride on believers, whom they think must surely always be in the wrong; they see their rights and their opinions rejected, which happens chiefly for the sake of God's Word and the faith of believers.

When they have accomplished it, they congratulate one another, boasting and bragging, as the Jewish leaders who conspired against the Nazarene did with Jesus. And yet, their terrible crucifixion revealed his resurrection; he accomplished everything he always intended. To their utter confusion, "he has put down the mighty from their thrones, and exalted those of low degree" (Lk 1:52).

Believe it or not, this happens among Christians as well. I used to follow the social media posts of a "friend" who would buy gift cards and gaming systems at Christmas—with his own nominal income, he pointed out—to give to the less fortunate. With his phone, he filmed himself offering a short sermon about how important it is to give back, and "the reason for the season," before walking into a fast-food place or dollar store and talking himself through choosing who looked the neediest. Then he shocked them, of course, by publicly presenting them the gift, telling them he was pastor at so-and-so church, and inviting them and everyone watching to attend there. Then he posted it on social media.

Presumably, he was attempting to offer a teaching moment or a heart-warming example of Christmas generosity to grow church attendance. But every time I saw one of those videos I was struck by how degrading to both the giver and the recipient they appeared. Because the recipients were being filmed, they seemed to feel required to be appropriately (effusively) humbled and thankful to the oh-so-generous man who had assumed their poverty.

And the giver seemed tone deaf to the recipients' uncomfortable thankfulness, since scads of "friends" liked or loved the post and commented on what a big heart he had and how lucky they were to have him as their pastor. I felt embarrassed, myself, watching those videos.

Perhaps his heart was entirely in the right place. But when we seek to exert influence in the Church by elevating ourselves to seem more holy or knowledgeable or successful than we are, or more holy or knowledgeable or successful than other people (Mt 23:1ff.), we become like the Pharisees who prayed aloud to be overheard or did good works in order to be seen and congratulated by others. And the Bible says they have received their reward in full (see Matthew 6:1–2).

Mary shows me a different way: when we acknowledge our lowliness, our dependence upon the might of God's arm, we receive through our weakness what we could never achieve in our own strength.

Let's Review

- "The strength of his arm" indicates *breaking of spiritual pride.*
- *God's strength begins where my strength ends.*
- My entire life is "bookended" between periods of helplessness (infancy and dying). *The true value of my lifespan is found in my willingness to embrace my utter helplessness with humility and faith.*
- Jesus redeemed even human "passion" (out-of-control emotions and desires) through his suffering and death (Acts 1:3). Both he and Mary reveal to me that the way of passion is the way of *deliberate vulnerability.*
- If I wait and trust long enough, *God will vindicate my faithful humility.*
- Mary's Magnificat teaches me that *the might of God's arm depends on what I express in receiving,* not on what I express in achieving.

Invitation

Surely you remember a time when you felt weak, helpless, or dependent on others. Maybe you also anticipate that for your future. Try to recall or imagine this circumstance. Then try the following LOVE the Word exercise. Let us pray.

God Prompt—LOVE the Word

L | Listen

"Three times I besought the Lord about this, that it should leave me; but he said to me, 'My grace is sufficient for you, for my power is made perfect in weakness.' I will all the more gladly boast of my weaknesses, that the power of Christ may rest upon me" (2 Cor 12:8–9).

O | *Observe*

Consider weakness. Reflect upon it. To whom does this verse apply? What does this verse mean? Where is the connection between our weakness and God's strength? When is God's power clearly seen? Why does Paul "boast of his weakness"?

In what circumstance in your life right now is God calling you to remain weak, in order that the strength of his arm may be revealed? Do you want to see him move mightily on your behalf? How do you need to change your approach in order to be obedient to this call? What might happen if you "pass over" with Jesus by purposely allowing yourself to remain weak? How is this approach like the "little way" of St. Thérèse of Lisieux?

V | *Verbalize*

Talk to God about your fears, concerns, and desires in the circumstance you named above. Ask him, with Jesus and Mary, St. Thérèse, and all the saints to help you rest deliberately in your weakness. Ask to see him work and move on your behalf.

E | *Entrust*

End your meditation by fully entrusting the circumstance to him. You may have to repeat this prayer many times as you wait on the Lord: "Jesus, I trust in you."

7

$\mathcal{H}$e Has Put Down ... and Exalted

(Luke 1:52)

Seeing the Hand of God at Work in Every Circumstance

In the last chapter we saw Mary declare, "He has shown strength with his arm" (Lk 1:51). In this, God reveals his power, revealing himself. In the process, he turns everything on its head, as Mary points out in the next verse of her Magnificat: "He has put down the mighty from their thrones, and exalted those of low degree" (Lk 1:52).

I think something is lost in the translation of the word *thrones*, which seems to imply that only kings and presidents and rulers are brought low. Rather, I like that the Douay-Rheims uses the word *seats*; all of us occupy some sort of seat of authority: leading a ministry or apostolate at church, managing projects or supervising people at work, parenting a child, or running a household. As adults, all of us possess some degree of authority.

I began learning about putting down and exalting when my husband and I were in a clown ministry at our denominational church before we were Catholic. Our little band of ministry members wore clown makeup and costumes, then performed spiritual skits to popular Christian music.

I was twenty-something, zealous and ignorant, and excited about what I thought was a great idea for a skit. So at one of our planning meetings, I proposed an idea and assigned parts for my new skit. The team seemed enthusiastic, and after a few weeks of practice, we performed the skit one Sunday evening to copious tears, raucous laughter, congratulations, and several rededicated lives at the altar call.

It turns out that not everyone was happy with what I had done. The husband-and-wife ministry leaders completely left the church, trailing murmurings of my clown ministry "takeover" that surfaced in the weeks afterward.

At first, I was angry at *their* immaturity, since they were at least twenty years older than I. I defended my motives vociferously to anyone who brought it up. But in my daily LOVE the Word practice, the Lord convicted me to humility. I began to see the situation from their point of view: I had never proposed my idea for the new skit to them before bringing it up in the meeting. Because of this, I had usurped their leadership and deeply offended them. What was more, I had stirred up division by causing people in the church to take sides, and I knew that God hates division and that peacemakers are blessed (see Proverbs 6:16–19, Matthew 5:9).

The nature of the accusations flying around made me hesitant to handle the matter privately, so I prayed for an opportunity to make things right. And then I left it in God's hands, relieved it was over. Heh, heh.

One Sunday night a few months later, the couple returned to our church for the first time. Pointed whispering began, and I was uncomfortable. When the pastor asked for testimonies after his sermon, several people stood to share praises and give testimony, and suddenly my heart began to pound with the knowledge that this was my opportunity.

At first I hoped the opportunity would pass as I waited, hoping that something would happen to make my testimony impossible. Finally, the church grew quiet; no one had anything else to say, and I knew I only had a few moments more to be obedient to God. I stood on trembling legs, turned to the couple, and apologized to God and everybody for my pride and my offense.

There was a loud, awkward silence for several minutes after I sat down, fighting back tears and thinking I was going to die. Then the pianist took up the closing song. I all but ran out of the church in humiliation.

A few weeks later it was necessary for the church to vote on who should serve on a new pastor selection committee, one of the most distinguished places of church service from our denomination. I was completely stunned when the secret ballots were tallied and the chairman of deacons announced that I had received more votes than anyone in the church. Had my husband not gotten almost as many, I would have served on that committee. Instead, I deferred to him so both of us would not be on the committee. Then I hurried out of the church, humbled again.

In my experience, there has never been a time when I have lowered myself, or let myself be lowered, that God did not later exalt me somehow. And Mary shows me that my final vindication may, and probably will, be delayed into eternity. But the promises of God in Mary's

Magnificat, and throughout the scriptures, are irrefutable. He *will* vindicate the humble.

Whatever position we may occupy, we should heed Mary's observation, for she shows us that reality is not defined by human reasoning but by God's *Is-ness*—which is very different from our own. God is establishing his kingdom in an evil world: he treats me better than I deserve and teaches me to do the same for others.

The "Turning" of Suffering and Evil

When we were kids and my mom made decisions we didn't like, we would say, "But that's not fair!"

She always replied, "Life's not fair!"

Deeply embedded in the human soul is the conviction that evil and suffering are not fair, and we instinctively struggle and push back against the pain. In fact, the most common cop-out against God, religion, or Christianity is the existence of all the evil in the world.

But what about the evil in me? Doesn't the evil in me deserve acknowledgment and punishment? Doesn't my selfishness help to cause and to perpetuate all the evil in the world? How is it fair to see everyone's evil but my own or my own suffering to the exclusion of everyone else's?

The first woman, Eve, shows us that God allows suffering partly because human evil causes suffering; in a sense, we deserve it. But God shows the strength of his arm by redeeming suffering, sending Jesus into the world not just to make us nicer people but also to usher God's kingdom into a fallen world.

God does things forward, to our backward. For instance, a miracle might be defined as a breach of natural law. Miracles look like anomalies to us, but they don't necessarily contradict nature, only what is presently known to us of nature and reality. What if miracles are really part of the natural order that is simply too advanced for us to understand?

Time, as the most essential, most basic experience of the world, is fundamentally real. We experience time as one instant flowing into another instant, because that's how nature is. Time seems to be running out, moment by moment. Yet the activity of time, or reality, is the continual construction of the future from the present. When something's time has come, we might say it has *become*.

God has the power to change the becoming, the status quo. He put down the proud Saul from his royal throne by lifting up the humble shepherd boy, David, in his place; he replaced proud Haman with the humble Mordecai and elevated Esther in the place of Vashti.

Mary says God has done and does and will do the same in every age, and accordingly, the scriptures use these past tenses. *He has scattered, put down, exalted* are to be taken in the widest sense, as signifying any time—future, present, or past, according to Hebrew idiom.

Several Fathers think this originally refers to fallen angels; as I mentioned earlier, many Fathers also believe that the number of humans will eventually equal the number of fallen angels.[1] By extension, the Jewish scribes, Pharisees, and priests, intent on their own gain, were selfishly negligent of the welfare of the people.[2] Either way, "he has put down" signifies he does and he will put down.

God Is Faithful

In the days of David and Solomon, the royal stem and line of David was green and flourishing, splendid in glory, might, and riches, and famous in the eyes of the world. As time went on, the Jewish leaders—priests, scribes, and Pharisees—became selfish and negligent of the welfare of the people. As priests continued to usurp power, the royal line of David became impoverished and despised, widely regarded as a dead stem, until at last it was thought that no king descended from this line could ever attain to any great glory, despite whatever promise God had once made to David.

However, God's ways are not ours, and he had sent a sign long ago: the rod of Aaron that budded in the Old Testament tabernacle foreshadowed the resurrection of the priesthood. This sign predicted that one day the high priest's dead staff would flower in the Messiah. And "when the time had fully come," Christ was born of the despised stem, of the poor and lowly maiden (Gal 4:4). For "the LORD sees not as man sees; man looks on the outward appearance, but the LORD looks on the heart" (1 Sm 16:7).

He destroys and puts down the mighty and the great who, with their own strength and authority, vent their pride on the godly and weak, who suffer injury, pain, death, and all manner of evil at their hands. And just as he confronts those who must finally be punished and shamed for their pride, he comforts those who must suffer injury and evil for the truth and the Word. As much as he comforts the latter, he corrects the former.

All of this must be known and waited for in faith. The weeds crowd and choke the wheat for a time (see Matthew 13:36–43). He does not destroy the mighty as suddenly as they deserve but lets them go for a season, until their might has reached its highest point. But when their might has done so, God does not support it; neither can it support itself; it breaks down of its own weight without any crash or sound, and the oppressed are raised up, also without any sound, for God's strength is in them, and it remains when the strength of the mighty has fallen.

Therefore Mary does not say he breaks the thrones, but he casts the mighty from their seats. Neither does she say he leaves those of low degree in their low degree but that he exalts them. For while the earth remains, it is necessary that authority, rule, power, and seats also remain. But God will not endure indefinitely those who abuse their positions, who use things and people for selfish ends, and who turn against him to inflict injustice on those they rule. All history testifies that he puts down one kingdom and exalts another, lifts up one principality and casts down another, increases one people and destroys another.

Assyria, Babylon, Persia, Greece, and Rome—all assumed they would occupy their seats forever. Throughout history, the elite rich and intelligentsia occupy political seats and gather fiefdoms as large as their grasp, and it will always be so: "The kings of the earth set themselves, and the rulers take counsel together, against the LORD and his anointed" (Ps 2:2). For truth and right must ever be in conflict with the wise, the mighty, and the rich, that is, with the world, the flesh, and the devil.

But the Holy Spirit comforts us through the mouth of the mother of Jesus and persuades us not to be deceived or afraid. Let them be wise, mighty, rich, lacking all simplicity: it will not last! Unless a ruler loves his subjects and is concerned chiefly with how to uplift and improve his people and not how to live at ease, his case is hopeless; he rules unto his own destruction.

Selfishness in responsibilities toward others reveals the pride that says "me first, no matter what," and in so doing, it sets itself up against God, who rules backward to our forward: "so the last will be first, and the first last" (Mt 20:16), and "whoever would be great among you must be your servant" (Mt 20:26). Everyone who cannot rule from his seat in this way will be put down, while those under him who humble themselves before God will be exalted.

For God So Loved the World

Perhaps it is useful to explore what humility really is. I once served in music ministry with someone who had a spectacular voice and musical talent who made a habit of putting himself and his talent down whenever someone complimented him (which was often, because he is truly gifted). His deprecation was so obviously untrue it had the opposite effect. Is pretending not to be good at something we are good at really biblical humility?

Biblical humility is demonstrated in this: "For God so loved the world that he gave his only Son" (Jn 3:16). Love gives. Love gives with extravagant sacrifice when it benefits the other. Love treats others better than they deserve, without pretending the other deserves it and without rubbing the other's nose in it. The word *loved* in this passage is *agape*, or sacrificial love, and is closely related to the Greek word for grace, *karis*. Love is grace. Grace is love.

St. Paul's choice of Greek words in his description of love in 1 Corinthians, chapter 13, demonstrates the inter-related nature of humility, grace, and love. In this soaring passage describing real love, the word *love—agape*—is often translated "charity," from the root *karis*, for its Greek specificity. One common Greek word for love was *eros*, the word for physical desire. Another was *philos*, which suggested the love of friends. Because neither of these words came close to describing the love he wanted to communicate, Paul chose the relatively rare word *agape*, which describes a love based on a deliberate act of will on the part of the one who loves, rather than the deservedness of the one loved.

It's a selfless, expect-nothing-in-return, treat-them-better-than-they-deserve type of love. In our contemporary throwaway society that prompts us to get rid of difficult friends, family, or acquaintances, agape love is "unprovoked," Paul says. Real love puts up with people who would be easier to give up on, not blindly or naively, but even while recognizing their problems and failures. This is God's own love.

I once had a mentor who modeled this principle. She was constantly doing little things for other people, a lot like Thérèse of Lisieux's little way. If she bought coffee, she bought an extra to give away. I once admired her beautiful silver pen and she gave it to me. She bought the person's groceries in line ahead of her. She smiled at people all the time, on purpose.

When we love this way, we allow others to rise. We take the lower, humble place, as a gift to the other. We experience eternal life as the quality that it really is, rather than the quantity of time we imagine. This quality of life is God's own life, a quality Jesus called "bliss," or blessedness, in his Sermon on the Mount, which we now know as the Beatitudes. It is counterintuitive, backward, revolutionary, but it is bliss to live and love this way, especially from whatever seat we occupy. Those who rule like God rules, love like God loves.

The humble, or lowly, are happy to receive everything from God simply because he sends it, even mistreatment at the hands of bad bosses and authorities. That is not to say they participate in sin of any sort. But they do not clamor for first place; rather, they wait on God to exalt them. The powerless are not necessarily those who are despised and nothing in appearance, but those who are willing to be in such a state, especially if they have been forced into it for the sake of God's Word or righteousness (*righteousness* simply means "what is right").

Mary goes on to sing about God's revolutionary plan. How do you participate in the revolution? Surely, it sounds too high and lofty for daily life in the midst of jobs, family, and all of the rest that goes with this life. But the revolution happens from our seat, wherever we are, in the smallest acts of humility and love. He accomplishes everything from such lowly positions; as Pope Benedict XVI points out, "Only from the saints, only from God does true revolution come, the definitive way to change the world."[3]

In one of my favorite passages in the Bible, St. Paul talks about this revolution and God's reasons for it:

> Rather, God chose the foolish of the world to shame the wise, and God chose the weak of the world to shame the strong, and God chose the lowly and despised of the world, those who count for nothing, to reduce to nothing those who are something, so that no human being might boast before God. (1 Cor 1:27–29, NABRE)

God will not tolerate our boasting forever. *Lowly* is the same expression Mary applied to herself. When he exalts the lowly, it does not necessarily mean that he will put them in the seats of those he has cast out, any more than when he shows mercy to them who fear him, he puts them in the place of the learned or proud. He grants them instead to be exalted spiritually and in himself, sometimes only in eternity, and to be judges over seats and powers, both here and in heaven, for they have more knowledge than all those who are wise and occupy some position.

Mary's Magnificat shows us that we ought gladly to be poor in spirit, to be wrong and let our adversaries be right. They will not continue in it forever; God's promise is too strong for them. They cannot escape God's arm, but they must succumb and be brought as low as they were once high, if we will simply believe and wait. Where there is no faith in his arm, God does not perform such works, but only when we lower our rights or opinions and suffer God's power and timing working in us. What precious works are these.

Those who depend on themselves prevent God's action in and through them. Mary's secret is that humility like hers unleashes the power of the Holy Spirit in the world: by God's action she was made the participant of a grace so immense that his gifts were extended through her to the whole world in every generation.

Mary recognizes his revolutionary presence. She proves that God works in secret ways of weakness to accomplish the great movements of his heart, and her Magnificat reminds me that in the turmoil of evil and suffering, God is quietly turning everything right-side-up with sacrificial love.

Let's Review

- *God promises to humble the proud and to exalt the lowly.*
- God chose Mary to bear "the flowering rod of Aaron," the long-awaited Messiah, *not because of her exalted station but because of her lowly heart.*

- *God does not often immediately destroy the proud*, but lets them go for a season until they fall under the weight of their own designs.
- *Those who rule like God rules, love like God loves.*
- *Agape love is God's own love,* a quality of life Jesus called "bliss."

An Invitation

I think one of the most pervasive impediments to going all-in with God is the fear we will lose ourselves by doing so. Indeed, the enemy tells us this awful lie as soon as he discerns we might be considering following God with all our heart, soul, mind, and strength. And yet what we miss in our unwillingness to be humbled is the exaltation he intended for us all along. Let us pray.

God Prompt–LOVE the Word

L | Listen

> Then the eyes of both were opened, and they knew that they were naked; and they sewed fig leaves together and made themselves aprons. And they heard the sound of the LORD God walking in the garden in the cool of the day, and the man and his wife hid themselves from the presence of the LORD God among the trees of the garden. But the LORD God called to the man, and said to him, "Where are you?" And he said, "I heard the sound of thee in the garden, and I was afraid, because I was naked; and I hid myself." ... And the LORD God made for Adam

and for his wife garments of skins, and clothed them. (Gn 3:7–10, 21)

O | Observe

Imagine you are in the Garden of Eden, as Adam or Eve, just before these verses. What do you see around you? Are there animals? How does it feel in your skin? What's the climate like? What do you hear? What are you thinking? What does it feel like to walk with each other and with God "in the cool of the day"? What do you smell? What does that fruit taste like as its juice bursts onto your tongue?

Now, read the passage again.

Where, lately, have your eyes opened to sin? What do you feel now that you did not feel moments before you recognized or felt the consequences of that sin? What is different? Why are you afraid? As you hear God approaching for his daily walk with you, why are you hiding? What are you hiding? Do your fig leaves help? Hear him call your name. What will you do, now, with the death that follows sin?

V | Verbalize

What thoughts and emotions bubble to the surface as you read and meditate on this passage? Have you allowed God to clothe you with his sacrificial forgiveness? Talk to him about your thoughts and feelings. What does he want you to do?

E | Entrust

Tell him what you will do. End your meditation by offering him the fruit of this LOVE the Word exercise—what he wants you to do and what you resolve to do. Ask him for the grace to obey, to continue in obedience, and to leave outcomes to him.

8

$\mathcal{H}$e Has Filled the Hungry

(Luke 1:53)

God's Heart for the Empty-Handed

When God rescued the Chosen People from slavery in Egypt, they journeyed for forty years through the desert wilderness, experiencing flesh-and-blood enemies as well as physical hunger and thirst on their way to the Promised Land. Yet God had a purpose for this, which he declared to his people through Moses: "[I] humbled you and let you hunger . . . that [I] might make you know that man does not live by bread alone" (Dt 8:3).

Most of us can't imagine being subjected to real hunger or poverty: lack of government assistance or clean water or shelter, an endless cycle of going to sleep hungry and awakening to struggle for the basic necessities. Whatever Mary means by hunger in her Magnificat, we do not usually take seriously the thought that she means it for us. Yet we find hunger mentioned over and over in the Old Testament, the bitter fruit of famine and pestilence and warfare. Why would God allow such hardship to be visited on his people?

St. Paul, in his epistle to the Romans, reminds us, "We know that in everything God works for good with those who love him" (8:28), and throughout scripture we find that God can use even hunger for food to teach his people to rely more fully on him. Sometimes he must empty our hands and hearts so that he might fill them with something better. The Vespers antiphons declare, "If you hunger for holiness, God will satisfy your longing, good measure, and flowing over."

In the book of 1 Kings, we meet the widow of Zarephath; she and her son were starving, brought so low by famine and misfortune that they were preparing to die when they encountered Elijah. "Fear not," he tells the widow. "For thus says the LORD the God of Israel, 'The jar of meal shall not be spent, and the cruse of oil shall not fail, until the day that the LORD sends rain upon the earth'" (1 Kgs 17:13–14). Their hands were empty, and God filled them with bread.

This principle echoes the Old Testament psalmist:

- "I have been young, and now am old; yet I have not seen the righteous forsaken or his children begging bread" (Ps 37:25).
- "The young lions suffer want and hunger; but those who seek the LORD lack no good thing" (Ps 34:10).

In reading and studying the Bible, it helps to remember that the full spiritual significance of events in the Old Testament is only fully revealed through history in the New Testament and even after. In the words of St. Augustine, it is "not the old [covenant] which is abolished, but the new which is hidden even in the old."[1]

For instance, the Promised Land of the Old Testament (see Genesis 13:15)—the homeland that the Lord prepared for the Chosen People, which because of sin Moses and Aaron were prevented from entering (see Numbers 20:12)—is imaged in Hebrews 4, describing those who seek the Promised Land of heaven with God: "Therefore, while the promise of entering his rest remains, let us fear lest any of you be judged to have failed to reach it" (Heb 4:1).

As we read in the *Catechism*, "'The Law is a pedagogy and a prophecy of things to come.' It prophesies and presages the work of liberation from sin which will be fulfilled in Christ: it provides the New Testament with images, 'types,' and symbols for expressing the life according to the Spirit" (CCC 1964).

The Old Testament is preparation for the Gospel. For example, in the Old Testament hunger is described primarily in literal, physical terms. However, in the New Testament, hunger points to a longing that is primarily spiritual (without setting aside the previous physical meaning). For example, in Matthew 4, the literal hunger of fasting from food hones Jesus' spiritual focus, preparing him for public ministry as well as his redemptive suffering. He emptied himself so he could be filled (see Philippians 2:6–8). And to us as well, Jesus promised in his Sermon on the Mount, "Blessed are those who hunger and thirst for righteousness, for they shall be satisfied" (Mt 5:6).

This, too, is part of becoming a magnificat, of imaging the glory of God in the world and accomplishing his purposes for us. We see this truth in the life of Mary: First we must be emptied; we must experience the spiritual hunger that God allows in us. Only then are we able to receive his progressive revelation, the divine pedagogy.

Blessed Are the Hungry

This spiritual hunger for righteousness was the princi-
pal motivator for my seeking full communion with the
Church. And yet it was not the culmination of my spiritual journey but the first steps of an altogether new spiritual path. For example, as non-Catholics, my husband
and I had never heard teaching against contraception.
We had no idea that it was regarded as illicit through
most of Church history; nor were we familiar with the
inherent medical dangers of chemical contraception. We
had contracepted our entire marriage.

I learned and completely accepted historical Church
teaching on the subject, even as I continued to allow the
chemicals into my body. My reason for not practicing
what I knew to be the truth was simple: my husband was
not yet persuaded.

This began to weigh on me. Finally, supremely conflicted over my hypocrisy, I went to my spiritual director.
We knew Catholic teaching would never persuade him—
my becoming Catholic had already created difficulties in
our marriage—and so my director advised me to tell my
husband about the medical dangers without making any
sort of demands that would force him into a corner and
further away from the Church. And then he told me to
pray for God to bring about the obedience that would fill
my hunger for righteousness.

It was a long, uncomfortable wait. My husband
wouldn't budge. He acknowledged the dangers, and even
the immorality, of abortifacient chemical contraception.
However, he was even more afraid of another pregnancy.
We had just had a surprise baby (a happy surprise, but
a surprise nonetheless), and he didn't want any more
surprises.

I prayed. I hid a scapular under his side of the mattress. I went to adoration. And then, just like that, the recession hit. I was laid off from my full-time job, his hours were cut by half, and we could no longer afford forty dollars a month for the pill. We were forced by simple economics to try Natural Family Planning. I have been contraception-free since.

The Bible is full of God's promises for provision, but often we contrive and demand fullness from him or satisfy our hungers ourselves before hunger and need really arrive. We hoard provisions against future hunger and want so that we no longer have need of God and his works. *If you're not famished for spiritual things, chances are it's not because you have feasted and are satisfied but that you have snacked on junk food away from the true table.* When your soul is stuffed with small things, there is no room for the great.

If you don't have a hunger for God, perhaps it is because your god is your belly: "Their end is destruction, their god is the belly, and they glory in their shame, with minds set on earthly things" (Phil 3:19).

God Fills Us with Himself

In thinking of how God fills the hungry, I particularly love the story of Abraham's call, because I especially relate to his reaction to God's word. In Genesis 12 Abram first experiences God, privately and intimately. Immediately afterward, he faces many seemingly unrelated challenges that appear to negate all he has heard from God. Nothing has worked out the way he thought, and the promise God gave him is still nowhere to be found; there is no child on the horizon. Instead, Abram faces back-to-back conflicts, confrontations, and dangers. After this extended

bout of activity Abram needs refreshment. He is depleted
and empty. He is hungry for affirmation, encouragement,
assurance. He needs more of God.

Abram's need brings God to him. The Lord fills
Abram with a mystical experience of himself through a
renewal of the covenant. "After these things the word of
the LORD came to Abram in a vision, 'Fear not, Abram,
I am your shield; your reward shall be *very* great.' But
Abram said, 'O Lord GOD, what wilt thou give me, for I
continue childless, and the heir of my house is Eliezer of
Damascus?'" (Gn 15:1–2, emphasis added).

The word *very* means "vehemently, exceedingly,
urgently." *Great* comes from the root meaning "increase,
heap up, multiply, abundant, bless." Together they con-
vey that the Lord your God is your furiously increasing
reward, your exponentially multiplying abundance.

As I read this account, I felt God was applying it to
me and the promises he had given me, so my question
was the same as Abram's: *Well, if this is true, that I will
receive some reward, what are you going to give me? What do
I get?* The Lord declared himself to be the reward: "*I am*
thy protector, and *thy reward exceeding great*" (Gn 15:1,
DRB, emphasis added).

Is that somehow deflating? Can you think of something else you would rather have than him? I confess at
first I was disappointed upon reading it. I had no concept
of how God himself could be any sort of reward. If that's
where you are, ponder Psalm 81:10: "Open your mouth
wide, and I will fill it."

Have you considered that you are already receiving a
reward? God is already giving himself to you. Right now
he is teaching you to trust him more implicitly through
Abram.

Anytime you apply yourself to the time and attention a contemplation like this requires and exercise the faith to apply what you learn, God will meet you in a shower of blessing. Nothing draws God like faith. He *must* act in the life of any person who offers him this irresistible invitation. Sooner or later, your God pursuit will be abundantly rewarded: "And without faith it is impossible to please him. For whoever would draw near to God must believe that he exists and that he rewards those who seek him" (Heb 11:6).

The rest of Genesis 15 contains a lot of peculiar practices that seem almost superstitious: cutting small animals in two, a burning torch passing through the pieces—but we are witnessing a formal covenant being wrought. In solemn agreements between ancient Semitic people, both parties of the agreement would pass between bloody pieces of slain animals and birds. It was like saying, "May I become like these torn animals if I do not keep my side of the bargain."

Notice how God had Abram prepare for the solemn ceremony of covenant making but only partly participate in it. God put Abram in what amounts to a spiritual ecstasy, told him of future events that would involve the tribe, and eventually the nation, to be made from him. He told Abram about the Egyptian slavery and exodus the Hebrew people would experience in years to come:

> Abraham's prayer is expressed first by deeds:
> a man of silence, he constructs an altar to the
> Lord at each stage of his journey. Only later
> does Abraham's first prayer in words appear:
> a veiled complaint reminding God of his
> promises which seem unfulfilled. Thus one
> aspect of the drama of prayer appears from

> the beginning: the test of faith in the fidelity of
> God (CCC 2570).

In answer to Abram's question of faith in God's integrity, God alone, in the form of smoke and fire, passed through the bloody animal carcasses. All Abram was required to do was prepare the offering. Abram was not required to walk the grisly pathway because the responsibility for the fulfillment of the covenant did not rest on his shoulders. God, in a solemn, formal swear, swore to bring it about himself. The fulfillment of God's promise to Abram, the Abrahamic Covenant, was as sure as the eternal life of the Lord.

In the emptiness, hunger, and poverty of Abram's childlessness, he received both God himself *and* the son he longed for. "He filled the hungry" with more than they could ever hold, but the rich are "sent empty away" (Lk 1:53), for they have need of nothing and are full of everything else.

Every Syllable Is Life

Have you considered that Jesus always, always said exactly what he meant, with no exaggeration, sarcasm, or idle chat? Why do we not believe him when he says,

- "Woe to you that are rich" (Lk 6:24) and
- "You cannot serve God and mammon" (Mt 6:24) or
- "It is easier for a camel to pass through the eye of a needle than a rich man to enter the kingdom of God" (Mat 19:24) and
- "Blessed are those who hunger" (Mt 5:6)?

Jesus' word is so powerful that it accomplishes every syllable of what he speaks (see Isaiah 55:11). He cannot utter a single false word or else work against himself. He means *every* word.

When Jesus requires his followers to give up all they possess, then, does he really mean it (see Luke 14:33)? Although I am not arguing against temperance as a virtue, notice he does not say eat, drink, spend, and consume *in moderation.*

Is he speaking of hunger figuratively? Does he simply mean a *spirit* of poverty? Does he mean we are to throw ourselves into the hopelessness of those in ragged clothes, with distende Just Released! Carla Cooke - Daughter of Legendary Sam Cooke d bellies, surrounded by flies and disease? That may be true for some. St. Teresa of Calcutta was called to such radical poverty. Does it not seem unjust for anyone to live in destitution when we in the West, and especially in the United States, are defined by the American dream of prosperity?

Are you irritated by the suggestion that Jesus means self-indulgent spending sends one to hell? I am not speaking in mere humanistic or sociological terms. I speak person to person, as a fellow Westerner indoctrinated in consumerism from birth. Listen to this:

> It can be argued that the single dominating and organizing value in American culture is economic—the good life. Our American culture promotes and rewards this and thereby educates to it. Even our universities have capitulated to this value. Too often they simply train for the job market. Practically, then, this means that other values will be pursued and promoted only within this overriding priority. Thus justice . . . is promoted within the dominance of the financial criterion—"if we can afford it," where

"afford" refers to the retention of a high level
of consumership.[2]

Exactly.

How much of our almsgiving is according to what
we can afford and not "What does God want?" "What am
I called to?" or "What is the need?"

How much of a sacrifice is required in order for me
to contribute at my current levels of tithing and almsgiving? Do I live frugally on purpose, in order to share
with others? Without exception, the saints lived a radical
evangelical poverty and are the best examples we have of
Jesus' true meaning of hunger and poverty as it applies
to priestly life, religious life, *and* married life.

The Hunger of the Saints

St. Robert Bellarmine, archbishop and cardinal, warned,
"It is certain that the bishop would sin mortally if, not
content with a frugal table and modest furnishings, he
fails to spend what money remains on the upkeep of his
churches and the sustenance of the poor."[3]

St. Francis Borgia was gluttonous far beyond the
point of obesity, yet in a conversion to the radical call of
Gospel hunger, he repented of overeating and slimmed.[4]

St. Bernard admonished, "Whatever goes beyond
bare nourishment and simple plain clothing is sacrilege
and theft."[5]

St. Liguori, in teaching on what in our day would
be considered unreasonable austerity, quotes St. John
Chrysostom to have taught that personal adornment was
opposed to Gospel hunger: "Attention to the ornaments
of the body indicates internal deformity." He also quotes

St. Thomas as saying, "It is good to give your goods to the needy, but it is better to be poor with Christ."[6]

Because I have an affinity for shabby chic-style, I particularly love Teresa of Avila's comment that she wanted her convents arranged and fixed up "with everything left rough and unpolished," so they could be lived in and not harmful to the health, but no extras.

Few want to believe or hear it, much less live it, but the saints are unanimous. A cursory read of Butler's *Lives of the Saints* will convict you to Mary's radical hunger with the greatest of uneasy pleasure.

The most radical of the saints were hungry unto destitution, yet they were always filled. The confessor of St. Catherine of Siena (a saint in a class by herself) wrote that her habitual fasting eventually reached a state of complete abstinence in which she lived entirely on the Eucharist and yet was "always bursting with life and happiness."[7]

And herein is the real lesson I believe.

The Bread of Life

As a non-Catholic, I prayed, *Lord, is there not some way we can be closer?* How could I have ever dreamed he might—or even could—answer my deepest hunger with his own Body, Blood, soul, and divinity, every single day at Mass? What kind of love is this?

This hunger for love is foundational to all other hungers and is one he alone can satisfy: "I am the bread of life. He who comes to me shall not hunger" (Jn 6:35). For so many of us, life is a succession of broken relationships and loveless experiences. In the West we seek entertainment over connection: elegant dining and drinking, wasted hours binging on Netflix or Amazon Prime. We seek out all kinds of love substitutes in order to satisfy that inner craving: trashy romance novels, casual sexual encounters, porn, and obsessive acquisition of possessions and wealth in a vain attempt to live up to what other people think. We take pride in position, possessions, birth, rank, education, social standing, extensive wardrobes, expensive traveling, prestige, and pleasure seeking. Yet all these things are impediments to love.

The saints' examples make it clear that understanding Gospel hunger properly requires a complete conversion, a 180-degree change of direction from worldly pursuits. The rich, full man, blinded by his attachments, not only doesn't do what he should with his wealth but he also does not even see Lazarus at his doorstep every day. Is it any wonder, then, that Jesus said, "It is easier for a camel to go through the eye of a needle than for a rich man to enter the kingdom of God" (Mt 19:24)?

To the rich man, bursting barns mean he should build bigger to eat more, drink more, entertain more (see Luke 12:16–21). Like Ebenezer Scrooge, it never occurs to him that his abundance is meant to be shared with those in his employ, the beggar at his door.

Who are the poor in your employ? Who is the beggar at your door?

What Mary's Hunger Is Not

We know that evangelical hunger is not laziness, carelessness, disorder, dirt, or unwillingness to work (see 2 Thessalonians 3:10). We are not being asked to give up basic necessities, as Mary did in giving birth in a cave. That was an extraordinary gesture—a sign for those who needed to find her little miracle (see Luke 2:12).

No, Gospel hunger requires that we share with the needy but not necessarily *be* needy. There may be seasons and circumstances where we may be called to that for a time, to be hands and feet for Jesus toward the poor and hungry. But this, too, is an extraordinary sign.

"He has filled the hungry with good things" (Lk 1:53). What was the nature of Mary's hunger in her Magnificat? Certainly not the selfish economy of Ebenezer Scrooge, who would never use his money for his own or anyone else's benefit, whether from fear or simple greed. And surely biblical hunger is not inattention to one's health or cleanliness (although the self-indulgent pampering that passes for self-care in America would likely scandalize the saints). The Church never seeks for saints among those who live comfortable lives. Rather, she always looks for evidence of Mary's hunger.

What is this Gospel hunger? It is partly detachment from riches and superfluities. It is an availability of one's person, time, and talent—along with good stewardship. It is not mere spiritual rhetoric, the stuff our pastors and bishops offer us to cajole us into giving generously without offending our self-indulgent spending.

Talking about the needy without sharing sacrificially with them betrays a dead faith (see James 2:14–17).

"No one can serve two masters," Jesus said. We must always choose the force that will direct our lives: God or money; one cannot have both (Mt 6:24). The Word of God is smothered, choked, and fruitless in anyone preoccupied with the cares—the pleasures, notoriety, and wealth—of this world (see Luke 8:14).

Mary's treasure was not on earth, where moths and rust corrode and thieves rob. Her treasure was in her womb, a womb filled for its emptiness and willingness to remain empty if it pleased God. Her treasure was in heaven, from whence Jesus came, and he gave himself to her, filling her completely. This same expectation is, in

Jesus her Son, our new axis (see Matthew 6:19–21). "He has filled the hungry" (Lk 1:53).

Remain Lighthearted

So what is hunger, really? If there is value in Gospel hunger, what is it? What is the value of negative things, as in the deficiencies of "the blessed" in the Beatitudes?

The value of Gospel deficiency is received from something positive, some sort of potential: the emptiness that anticipates, welcomes, and *needs* a filling. Hunger offers not simply an abstract idea but a concrete experience of openness. Of course, openness is relative: some yield nothing, but some yield thirty, sixty, or a hundred-fold fruit.

Biblical hunger, though, embraced in faith, transforms one in the deepest seat of his being. It grows and fills him, makes him open to whatever Jesus wants to communicate. How will I know what Jesus wants to communicate to me when I am closed to him, drowsy by the preference and satisfaction of distractions and pleasures?

> But take heed to yourselves lest your hearts be weighed down with dissipation and drunkenness and cares of this life, and that day come upon you suddenly like a snare; for it will come upon all who dwell upon the face of the whole earth. But watch at all times, praying that you may have strength to escape all these things that will take place. (Lk 21:34–36)

The weight of drowsiness is that of being stuck in sin, of seeking to satisfy, by ourselves, the human hunger for love and life. The cares of life Jesus refers to may be concerns over living up to our expectations of life, concerns of living every possible experience, preoccupation with satisfying our hungers on our own. Some indulge in the momentary delight of drunkenness, only to find themselves a little more damaged afterward. Dissipation is amusement, entertainment, possibly to excess, but always the effort to numb, to entertain, to fill the God-sized hole.

Others attach themselves to different inclinations but to identical results, which Christ defines as a sad heart, a heavy heart. The promise of fullness is formidable for those with hearts heavy with dissipation and drunkenness and worries of life. These hearts are opaque, dull, and resistant to God's Word.

The detached, the little ones, and the hungry are so open and ready for filling that they somehow already possess it. They possess him. No one surrounded by luxury, comfort, pleasure, entertainment, prestige, and position, who lives only for the good opinion of neighbors, is open to Mary's radical filling. Mary shows me that detachment is half of openness; humility is the other.

All of us are to be open, ever ready to receive from God like Mary. We are to be like lilies, uncluttered, simple, receiving everything, blooming where we are planted, knowing from whom we came and to whom we go and how quickly that happens. Like her, we are unconcerned about food or drink or clothes. We detach ourselves from these worries and set out hearts exclusively on him and the kingdom he sets up in us (Mt 6:25–34). All of the saints were not only willing to be stripped of all possessions, but they rejoiced in the privilege, since it aligned them more closely with their savior who always rewards those who throw their lot in with him.

The connection between riches and attachment is obvious to anyone who has come into possession of something he is reluctant to part with, even when someone else needs it more than he. If you are concerned about whether your possessions possess you, then give them away. That's the only way you can ever know.

Mary's Magnificat shows us that hunger has a great deal to do with humility. We equate our identity, who we are, with what we have: education, influence, portfolio, possessions. She had none of it.

Neither is the greatest of all poverty material rather than spiritual, as St. Teresa of Calcutta emphasized. What does it profit, then, to gain the entire world but lose one's soul? Mary's view of hunger and emptiness is a matter of eternity for us.

Without action, faith is dead. Words are cheap and multiple, but action is costly. The saints are full to over-flowing in action: things are means; people are ends. To use possessions as an end in themselves is to make a god of our stuff. Paul says eating, drinking, and all else should be done solely for the glory of God, which must always be inseparable from our own good (see 1 Corinthians 10:31). Gospel hunger uses things in a way that one can honestly say we have given glory to God.

The Currency of Eternity Is Love

Hunger and poverty, it is true, are not found in heaven. Poverty abounds here, among the lush wealth of the earth. A single seed of corn bears not one kernel a year but thousands of them. A frog lays not one or two or three eggs but hundreds and hundreds of them. Uncountable, unrecorded, undiscovered species of flora and fauna thrive in unseen crevices of the earth. The subatomic activity of our world agitates with activity too small to see. The universe teems with galaxies on a scale of light-years and billions upon billions of stars that humanity can never comprehend.

Is it right to be hungry when the earth produces more food that can be eaten, more food thrown away than is eaten? Yet amid all the wealth and fullness of earth, hunger and poverty abounds. Only when the Lord came down from heaven and chose it for himself, to make it precious to us, was it redeemed. Only then did we learn its value.

Why all the guts and roaring about the wealth of the poor and hungry, then? Gospel hunger assumes that true satisfaction is found in love. In people, not things, and especially the divine person. Would it not serve me better to clear out the space for him to fill me with that fullness for which every human creation stretches toward?

This is why the saints write so much about detachment: because they write and live so much about love. Those who want no part of hunger or poverty want no part of love. Nowhere in scripture are we asked for most of, much, or a lot. Always, we are asked for everything. It's as though Jesus says, "I will think of everything. You think only of loving me."

God is not a God of fractions or percentages. Blessed are the hungry and empty are the rich because the hungry suffer no impediment to what they most deeply crave: Jesus' love in their depths, depths deeper than the belly. Never have I been more happy or at peace than the times in my life when I was most spiritually and financially empty while trusting completely in him to fill the holes.

Mary, the queen of the saints of love and doctors of prayer, knows with all of them that there is no delight, no created pleasure, equal to the absorption in, the complete possession by, and the union with divine love. Once you have tasted of such, the soul longs for it to the exclusion of all else. Should the soul find itself reattached and possessed by things, the soul languishes until it gives it up and falls into the embrace of its lover once again. These are the hungry who experience the eucharistic mysteries fully, burning with love (*Sacrosanctum Concilium* 10).

Perhaps especially for us in the West, who are so caught up in the never-ending pursuit of "more," only God can work the conversion that prompts the wealthy man to give away what he does not need. But this biblical hunger offers a unique type of freedom, in which one is disposed to union with God: complete filling, filling up, filling out, filling in. Jesus promises, "I am the bread of life; he who comes to me will not hunger, and he who believes in me shall never thirst" (Jn 6:35).

What is this freedom, exactly? Mary shows us the power of simplicity, what spiritual hunger is. Her example points out how contemporary consumerism squashes the desire and faith necessary to see God provide miraculously in our lives. "Having nothing, and yet possessing everything" (2 Cor 6:10).

God will not force himself on me. If I cling to things and attachments, he lets me have my things and attachments. Mary assures me that if I am empty of things he fills me with himself in ways and to depths and satisfaction and satiation that eyes have not seen and ears have not heard (see 1 Corinthians 2:9).

The hungry are filled, indeed. They have everything.

Let's Review

- *Old Testament hunger was primarily physical, while New Testament hunger is primarily a spiritual longing* (without negating the physical effects).

- *We must experience spiritual hunger in order for God to fill us.*
- If you are not hungry for God, *what poor substitute is filling you up?*
- *Simplicity is powerful* because it frees me to receive more of God.
- *If I have not seen God provide miraculously for me, perhaps I have not risked* hunger with him.
- *The currency of heaven is love.*

Invitation

As I was researching my way into the Church and my knowledge of the faith was growing, I became more and more hungry for the day I would receive Jesus in the Eucharist. When the Easter Vigil finally arrived, it was a supermarital moment in which I recognized his complete self-donation for me and the answer to my deepest prayer of longing to be closer to him. In the Eucharists since then, I grow hungrier and hungrier to make my own self-donation to him fuller and fuller. Let us pray.

God Prompt–LOVE the Word

L | Listen

"Jesus said to them, 'I am the bread of life; he who comes to me will not hunger, and he who believes in me shall never thirst'" (Jn 6:35).

O | Observe

On a daily basis, as you approach each meal, do you allow yourself to get hungry or do you eat something as soon as you feel the early pangs?

Practice delaying your meals to allow yourself to get hungry before you eat. As you do so, and especially as you fast, pay attention to your hunger pangs. Ask yourself, *In my world, what am I most hungry for—right now, this year, for the rest of my life?* Be specific. Perhaps just the question has every hunger you've ever experienced surfacing, leaping out of the water like spawning salmon. You may answer: "I want a gallon of Rocky Road ice cream." And maybe that's true on the surface. But what's under that desire? Are you actually hungry, bored, or sad instead? Can a gallon of ice cream relieve any of those deeper longings? Why are you bored? Why are you sad?

Maybe the first question is, *What am I really hungry for?* But to get deeper and know what we yearn for, we have to keep asking why till we get all the way to the bottom of the desire. It's very important to know what a true hunger is, because that may actually be what God wants to give us.

V | Verbalize

Talk to him about your desires and longings until you get to the bottom of what you're really hungry for. Ask God for that, because "he rewards those who seek him" (Heb 11:6). The original Greek for *seek* implies a diligent search and even demand. What do you need to do to diligently seek him?

E | Entrust

Receive the Eucharist with the intention that God might satisfy your hunger. Pray for that intention and thank him for the answer to that prayer, before you see the answer, as you kneel in his presence after Communion.

9

*H*e Has Helped His Servant Israel

(Luke 1:54)

Remembering God's Merciful Gaze

The Gulf War was in full swing; sentiments and fears were running high. We were in public, and I heard a woman angrily disparaging people from the Middle East with blanket statements while she talked about her faith and Christianity in general. I thought she would swallow her tongue when a bystander looked at her and told her she was going to be decidedly uncomfortable in heaven with Jesus, who is Hebrew: Middle Eastern with features like Muslims and Arabs.

This point really came home to me during my first pilgrimage to the Holy Land. I wanted this to be a true pilgrimage, so I chose a date and went by myself with a group of strangers. We were met by our guide, who looked intently at me and said, "You have our blood." How right he was. At the time, he meant Mediterranean blood, but we Christians all share the Blood of Christ.

41

Early in the week of the pilgrimage we went to the Sea of Galilee, got on a "Jesus boat" and traveled to the other side of the sea, just as Jesus and his disciples had done numerous times. Our captain and crew raised the American flag to fly alongside Israel's flag during our national anthem and then played praise music as we made our way to the other side.

At some point I was relatively alone on the bow of the boat. I threw my arms open wide in the *Titanic* stance and praised the Lord with the music blaring, in thanksgiving for the gift of the trip. I thanked him for how beautiful the Holy Land is and how amazing it felt to be on the same water he had walked on.

I almost fell off the boat when he replied to my thanksgiving: "I just wanted you to see *my place.*"

Jesus has a place? I was so struck by that. But of course he does! The Incarnation is the tuning fork of time, and if it is true that Jesus is a man, then he lived in a place. The Divine Man, sure, but a real flesh-and-blood man who lived in a definite place.

The Three Israels

When Mary praises God's remembrance of Israel in her Magnificat, she looks back at the long history of her people. She is in "his place" because it is her place; it is, on earth, the place of God's people, forever. But she also looks forward to the final place, that Promised Land of heaven where all of God's people—past, present, and future—will be gathered into one body and one place.

Israel #1, Jacob

The Bible speaks of Israel in three ways: first, in the person of Jacob, whose name was changed to Israel in a renewal of the Abrahamic covenant handed down to him from his grandfather, Abraham, and his father, Isaac.

The story of Jacob's name change is in Genesis 32, where Jacob is assaulted by a strange man who engages him in a prolonged struggle, wrestling with him all night beside the river Jabbok, a name derived from the root for "failure." Jacob was strategically alone by the river after having sent his caravan and all his defenders ahead.

This was a man truly alone, having estranged his own family. As we read his story, we witness his extended lack of integrity in scheming to rule over his brother and deceive his father. Jacob was born a deceiver: his name means "supplanter." He gets away with conniving for a long time, until one day God confronts Jacob and wrestles with him over his integrity through an angel.

The story is told from Jacob's point of view, and yet it becomes apparent that the angel could have bested him at any moment when he puts Jacob's thigh out of joint as a demonstration of definitive superiority. The wound leaves Jacob limping after the battle as a reminder of the reality and intensity of the struggle. Jacob was not crazy; the fight and the wound were real.

Such foul play may make one sympathize with Jacob, but as the Genesis account later reveals, it was the angel of God with whom Jacob actually wrestled. Surely the angel could have simply spoken a word and struck Jacob dead rather than expend the effort and time in a seemingly useless struggle.

The text does not say so, but I believe Jacob discovered something about his adversary through the course of this intense midnight struggle; he demanded a blessing before the stranger left, and with more than a little respect conveyed in the telling, the angel indeed blesses and tells him, "for you have striven with God and with men, and have prevailed" (Gn 32:28).

This fascinates me. How on earth is it possible to wrestle with God? How does one win a struggle with the God of the universe? Why would God stoop to undertake such a silly striving that is no match for his unequalled power?

Interestingly, Jacob never asks why he was confronted and opposed, he simply asks to know the man's name. Then the angel says something mysterious: "Why is it that you ask my name?" (Gn 32:29) and the name remains undisclosed.

To ask one his name in that time was to ask who the person was. A name was not simply a title; it revealed a person's character and nature. And so, when the angel acquiesced to Jacob's request for a blessing, the angel asked, "What is your name?" In asking for Jacob's name, the angel wanted a confession of his character.

"Jacob" (supplanter). The moment Jacob confessed his name—the moment he was brutally honest about himself—coming face to face with who he was and face to face with him with whom we all have to do—a supernatural transformation began. Jacob's theophany became an epiphany.

Jacob's willingness to be pierced to the division of soul and spirit and joints and marrow allowed the thoughts and intentions of his heart to be laid open (see Hosea 12:4). Wholeness of heart was accomplished by the Word of God, and Jacob's integrity was achieved through his confession. Suddenly he was no longer "supplanter" but *Israel*, meaning "prince with God."

This inscrutable episode changed Jacob and became the defining moment in his spiritual life. Hosea 12:4 reports there were tears of unsuccessful exertion involved in Jacob's supreme struggle that night. He moved forward in humility and blessing to fulfill what had been promised him many years earlier.

I imagine the sudden failure of his thigh by the finger of the "man" was supremely discouraging, as he would have known the angel could have won at any time and was simply condescending to Jacob's weaker effort.

The Hebrews used the word *thigh* to denote the reproductive organs. The ability to reproduce was so important, that area was used, symbolically, as collateral in covenant making, so that to forge a covenant it was customary to put one's hand under the thigh of the one requiring him to swear. Therefore, to strike the hip or thigh was to indicate complete superiority (see Judges 15:8). Jacob was made to know he had been utterly conquered, even as he received the covenant from the angel. How, then, could it be said he had won?

It wasn't very long ago I found myself beside the chaotic waters of failure. Devastated, with my confidence rattled senseless and to the core, I did battle with God there in my midnight. I exerted all my heart, soul, mind, and strength in the effort. Deeply hurt, I began repeating his own words back to him, almost sarcastically, all the things God had said to me that had led me, yet again, to make that humiliating failed attempt.

I, like Jacob, knew something about God, even as I wrestled with him: I know he loves me, and I know he is good. While I did not understand the struggle at all, I all but demanded the blessing through my raw and painful tears. You know what? I got it.

Jacob was the first Israel, but he was only the beginning.

Israel #2, Jewish Nation

Genesis, the "book of beginnings," is largely about God's sovereign work in the lives of the patriarchs for the good of all nations. Abram, before he was Abraham, was the first to be called a Hebrew (see Genesis 14:13), a designation that comes from the name Eber, who was Noah's great-grandson and a distant ancestor of Abraham (see Genesis 11:14–17). Eber, meaning "to cross over or pass through," died at the age of 464 when Jacob would have been seventy-nine. When the angel of the Lord changed Jacob's name to Israel, Jacob then became the personification of the Jewish nation.

Thereafter, God revealed himself as "the God of Abraham, the God of Isaac, and the God of Jacob" (Ex 3:6), and the family of God became known as Hebrews or Israelites. Through Moses, the Israelites became a nation. According to Dr. Scott Hahn, in something like increasingly large concentric circles, God's people grew with each of his six progressive covenants: with man and wife through Adam and Eve; with family through Noah; with tribe through Abraham; with nation through Moses; with kingdom through David; and with universe through Christ.[1]

Abraham's covenant was renewed with his son Isaac and Isaac's son Jacob, whom God later renamed Israel, so that Jacob's sons were the original "children of Israel." That family of twelve squabbling sons went on to father the twelve tribes of Israel, who lived not yet in the place promised to Abraham, the Promised Land, but as slaves under the Egyptian pharaohs of the great pyramids.

As the innumerable people of God labored under their Egyptian masters, they cried out for deliverance: "God heard their groaning, and God remembered his covenant with Abraham, with Isaac, and with Jacob" (Ex 2:24). He sent them a Hebrew kinsman who had grown up in Pharaoh's palace, specially prepared by God to deliver them.

Eventually the nation of Israel rejected God's leadership through the priests, judges, and prophets, and wanted a king like their neighboring nations (see 1 Samuel 8). A young warrior-poet-shepherd boy whose heart was known and chosen by God would be the second king of Israel and next covenant steward. David was anointed and then formed in the crucible of persecution for fifteen years before he ascended the throne. He reigned for forty years, unifying the Israelites under one ruler and conquering surrounding nations through near-constant military campaigns. He remains the most honored and acclaimed king of Israel's history.

God's covenant with David was the promise of an eternal dynasty. Ultimately, a righteous king greater than David was coming. He would be David's "son," or descendant, and would rule from David's throne forever (see 2 Samuel). The promise was confirmed in Psalm 89 and repeated to Solomon, David's son (see 1 Kings 9:5). This promised king is Jesus.

Israel #3, the Universal People of God

Many years after David, the prophets foretold a new, complete, final covenant that would include both Jews and Gentiles, indeed the whole world: the one, holy, catholic (meaning universal), and apostolic church: "But this is the covenant which I will make with the house of Israel after those days, says the LORD: I will put my law within them, and I will write it upon their hearts" (Jer 31:33).

How do we know that these Old Testament prophets were speaking of a covenant that extended not only to the Jews but to the Gentiles as well? Ezekiel prophesied it would be an eternal covenant (see Ezekiel 37:26). Isaiah was shown its universal character, so "that my salvation may reach to the end of the earth" (Is 49:6). In what is called a Servant Song for its prophetic nature regarding the Messiah, Isaiah also saw that the new covenant would be a person: "I have given you as a covenant to the people, a light to the nations" (Is 42:6).

From the beginning of his ministry, the Lord Jesus instituted the Twelve as "the seeds of the new Israel and the beginning of the sacred hierarchy" (CCC 877). In John 10, the Good Shepherd discourse, Jesus himself spoke of the "other sheep, that are not of this fold": "I must bring them also, and they will heed my voice. So there shall be one flock, one shepherd" (Jn 10:16). The boundaries of his sheepfold included not just the children of Israel but every nation under heaven (see Matthew 28:19).

The Church is the spiritual Israel or, in Catholic parlance, the "new Israel" (see CCC 877). Paul also takes up that theme. In Romans 9:6 he says that "not all who are descended from Israel belong to Israel." This indicates the existence of two Israels. One—"all who are descended from Israel"—indicates the ethnic people, not all of whom believe in Jesus.

According to St. Paul, the new Israel does not include those who have rejected the Messiah. Rather, the new Israel, founded by the Messiah, exists in spiritual continuity with the Old Testament saints and is a spiritual Israel. This spiritual Israel includes Gentiles who believe in the Messiah and who, through baptism, are spiritually circumcised (see Colossians 2:11–12) and counted as spiritual Jews (see Romans 2:26–29).

In several places in scripture, Paul is explicit about the Gentiles' spiritual inclusion when he states that "you Gentiles in the flesh . . . were at that time separated from Christ, alienated from the commonwealth of Israel. . . . But now in Christ Jesus you who once were far off have been brought near. . . . So then you are no longer strangers and sojourners, but you are fellow citizens with the saints" (Eph 2:11–13, 19).

Paul emphasizes that "For he is not a real Jew who is one outwardly, nor is true circumcision something external and physical. He is a Jew who is one inwardly, and real circumcision is a matter of the heart, spiritual and not literal" (Rom 2:28–29).

Christ himself is the new covenant between God and his people. In Latin, covenant is *convenire*, meaning "to agree" and "to come together." Indeed, it is the new coming together of God and his people in the person of Christ, our new covenant, that forges the universal people of God, Jew, and Gentile.

Signs of the New Covenant

The prophesied new covenant is the master theme of the New Testament that it is named for. When Paul explained the institution of the Eucharist at the Last Supper, his language indicates a whole body of tradition, teachings that he received from Christ and delivered to the Corinthians, even repeating Christ's own words:

> For I received from the Lord what I also delivered to you, that the Lord Jesus on the night when he was betrayed took bread, and when

he had given thanks, he broke it, and said, "This
is my body which is for you. Do this in remembrance of me." (1 Cor 11:23–24)

It is this Body of Christ, which we receive in the
Eucharist, that both strengthens us—just as the manna
strengthened the children of Israel in the desert—and
draws us together into a single body, the Church, which is
a visible sign of the new covenant, God's presence in the
world. Through the institution of the Eucharist and the
establishment of the Church, the promised Messiah that
the prophets had long foretold was definitively revealed
to the world.

The theme is reinforced in the letter to the Hebrews:
"This makes Jesus the surety of a better covenant" (Heb
7:22). There were Jews in Jesus' time who did not believe
he was the Messiah, and there still are. It seems to some
that God's way of placing Jesus definitively as the Messiah in Judaism was what Jesus foretold as the end of
the world as the Jews knew it (see Matthew 24:2): the
destruction of the Jewish Temple, the center and symbol
of Jewish life.

Jesus predicted that the old, stone Temple would
be completely leveled to clear its foundation for the new
temple, his body, and history bears him out. The destruction of the temple occurred in AD 70, and it has never
been rebuilt despite several efforts, the most notable by
the Roman emperor Julian the Apostate, whose work, it
is said by some, God miraculously halted.

The Church in Christ's body, then, is the "new Jerusalem" (Rv 21:2). But does that mean the Jewish people
have been cast off? Have all the eternal promises been
assumed by Gentiles? After all, Jesus himself and the

apostles, and every author of every book of scripture, except Luke, was Jewish.

Evidently, and curiously, not. God still has plans for the Jews as a unique people (see CCC 674). Paul clearly indicates so in his writings, especially in Romans 9–11, where he says God continues to fulfill his promises for the Jewish people by preserving a remnant of Jewish believers in Christ (see Romans 11:1–5). This indicates a special place for Israel, for no other people has a promise that there will always be a believing remnant.

According to Paul, one day the Jewish people as a nation will return to Christ (see Romans 11:12, 15). Their return will be one of the signs of the Second Coming and Four Last Things, including resurrection of the dead (see CCC 673–682). Until then, as our *Catechism* intones, "Israel is the priestly people of God, 'called by the name of the LORD,' and 'the first to hear the word of God,' the people of 'elder brethren' in the faith of Abraham" (CCC 63).

Pope John Paul II said it beautifully when addressing the Jewish people of his day,

> The Church of Christ discovers her "bond" with Judaism by "searching into her own mystery." The Jewish religion is not "extrinsic" to us, but in a certain way is "intrinsic" to our own religion. With Judaism, therefore, we have a relationship which we do not have with any other religion. You are our dearly beloved brothers and, in a certain way, it could be said that you are our elder brothers.[2]

All of us together at the last day, Jacob, the nation of Israel, and the whole people of God, "his servant Israel," will welcome and celebrate "in remembrance of his mercy, as he spoke to our fathers, to Abraham and to his posterity forever" (Lk 1:54–55). Indeed, God has remembered his mercy from the beginning of time, as the messianic genealogies of the gospels illustrate.

In Remembrance of His Mercy

The Jews constantly call the Messiah the "son of David." Matthew's genealogy stresses that Jesus is the expected Messiah promised from generation to generation by connecting him to the recipients of the messianic promises. From the birth of Abraham to the birth of Christ there were 2,000 years; from the death of David to Christ, 1,013 years. Both Matthew and Luke take great care to trace the antiquity of the oracles and promises concerning Christ. Mary, too, points out God's faithfulness in fulfilling them, here in her Magnificat.

Matthew carefully derives the genealogy of Christ from Abraham, even through forty-two generations, in order to show the Jews that Jesus Christ was the true Messiah promised to Abraham; that he was the Son of Abraham and the rest of the patriarchs; and that he should be received, cherished, and worshipped by the Jews.

Interestingly, in Matthew's genealogy of Christ, with the exception of his Blessed Mother, only four females are mentioned, three with less-than-perfect reputations— Tamar, Rahab, and Bathsheba—and the fourth, a Gentile, Ruth the Moabitess. As with Mary's Magnificat, the human genealogy of Christ serves to show the vanity of high birth and that true nobility consists not in ancestry but in our own noble disposition and virtue.

Luke's genealogy is universal and goes back to Adam, head of the human race. Descended from Adam and with no human father (see Luke 1:35), Jesus inaugurates a new human era, one of the spirit. After Adam, sin lives in humanity through original sin. But Jesus is the New Adam (see Romans 5:12), the image in which God remakes his creation. We sin after the pattern of Adam's transgression. But the grace won for us by Christ's obedience means that sin is no longer our master.

The two lists from David to Joseph have only two names in common. Luke arranges his into three sets of two-by-seven names that Matthew omits. St. Jerome offers that Luke wished to form three exact series of fourteen generations each. Both lists end with Joseph as Jesus' legal father because legal paternity is enough to establish hereditary rights, the rights of the messianic line. Jesus came to be of the royal line of David through Joseph's adoption at the prompting of the angel's word in a dream. The line will not be through Mary as long as her male heir is alive.

According to the Fathers, these holy ancestors rose and ascended with him in common with the rest of the patriarchs,[3] of whom Matthew said, "Many bodies of the saints who had fallen asleep were raised" (Mt 27:52).

Mary's father, Joachim, had no male children, a fact that Matthew here omits as something perfectly well known in the age in which he writes. Therefore, it was Mary's duty to marry a husband of her own tribe and family. The genealogy of Joseph became the genealogy of our Lady and consequently of Christ. The Fathers all teach Joseph and Mary were of the same tribe and family.

"Being obedient she became the cause of salvation for herself and for the whole human race," St. Irenaeus says, joining many of the early Fathers in calling Mary the New Eve: "The knot of Eve's disobedience was untied by Mary's obedience: what the virgin Eve bound through her disbelief, Mary loosened by her faith."[4] Mary is compared with Eve by Justin Martyr circa AD 150, Tertullian circa

AD 200, Augustine in about AD 400, and too many more to name; all call Mary "the Mother of the living" and frequently claim "Death through Eve, life through Mary." Mary is the dawn, and the dawn unfailingly announces the arrival of the sun.

Mary is the first New Testament witness of Matthew and Luke's "books of the generation," as St. John Chrysostom calls Jesus' genealogies, since that ancestry

> is the sum of the whole dispensation, the root of all its blessings; viz. that God become man; for this once effected, all other things followed of course. And do not consider this genealogy a small thing to hear: for truly it is a marvelous thing that God should descend to be born of a woman, and to have as His ancestors David and Abraham.[5]

We are the posterity of Mary's fathers; they are our fathers. Their lives witness to all Mary sings in her Magnificat, as do all the saints after them. To us all belong the help and inheritance of which Mary has sung.

Let's Review

- When Mary speaks of "his servant Israel," *she means God's people throughout salvation history.*
- *The Church is the "new Israel,"* a fulfillment of the new covenant under Christ (CCC 877).
- This new Israel exists in continuity with the Old Testament saints. *The Jewish people are our "elder brothers" in the faith* and share in our spiritual ancestry.
- The destruction of the Temple in Jerusalem in AD 70 fulfilled *the prediction of Christ that his body was the*

temple of the new covenant, fed through the Eucharist and established at his Word.
- Because we belong to the Body of Christ, *we are spiritual ancestors not only of the Holy Family but of Abraham and the Chosen People as well.*

Invitation

Mary's Magnificat reminds us of the profound, eternal importance of our placement into the family of God. By virtue of our baptism, we are heirs of the promises and blessings she celebrates in her heartfelt song.

Like the first Israel, Jacob; the nation of Israel as a whole; and the universal people of God, the new Israel; each of us finds ourselves confronted by nameless adversaries, people, and circumstances; we fight valiantly; we rage and cry and wail; our own character is used to engage and defeat and bless us; we are wounded and changed forever; we wonder what the heck is going on, why it's happening; and God does not answer us.

Who is he, this helper / opponent who seems to both empower us to fight and wound us to win? What kind of God does this?

Dear friend, isn't salvation a sweaty enterprise involving every strenuous labor and that will ultimately require your very last breath? The midnight striving is meant to wound but change you for the better, for it is always God with whom we ultimately wrestle. Mary points back to the long line of those before us who experienced it and forward to those we will also inspire, so that if not an immediate or direct answer, there is a solemn blessing in every struggle; you only have to ask. Let us pray.

God Prompt—LOVE the Word

L | Listen

"Jesus said to her . . . 'We worship what we know, for salvation is from the Jews'" (Jn 4:21–22).

O | Observe

Find a local synagogue and attend a Sabbath (Shabbat) service or watch a video online. Observe the similarities and differences between what constitutes Sabbath practice for the Jewish people and what your Sunday liturgy, worship, and practice look like. Imagine Jesus observing Sabbath like this.

V | Verbalize

Remembering that Mary and Joseph, Jesus, and the apostles were all Jewish, pray for the Jewish people, your "elder brothers" in faith. Offer your thoughts and feelings to God.

E | Entrust

Lord Jesus, let your prayer of unity become a reality for all believers, in your way. We pray and long for the day when we are one as you and the Father are one. Help us know when and how to cooperate in that unity. Amen.

10

$\mathcal{A}$s He Spoke to Our Fathers

(Luke 1:55)

Allowing the Word to Come Alive in Us

As the song draws to a close, Mary's Magnificat recalls how she heard God speak to her, just "as he spoke to our fathers" (Lk 1:55). Mary knows God continues in every generation to keep his promises. Pope Benedict XVI said, "Mary speaks with us, speaks to us, invites us to know the Word of God, to love the Word of God, to live with the Word of God, to think with the Word of God."[1]

Mary teaches us how to hear God speak "as he spoke to our fathers" and to her, how to love the Word the way she does, so that all of us lowly ones can experience the wonder of God's promises and powerful fulfillment in our own lives. In thinking about how he spoke to our fathers and how he continues to speak to us, I asked Mary to show me what she knows about this, how she observes God's Word to her, and I received an unexpected answer.

In an address in St. Peter's Square on May 31, 2013, Pope Francis followed Mary through the annunciation, where we witness her personal hearing practice, outlining how practically and beautifully she illustrates the traditional steps of lectio divina. She LOVEs until the Word of God comes alive within her and is born into the world, and she wants us to know how to do the same. (We have been practicing her method together in each chapter's "God Prompt.")

First, Mary listens to the Word of God.

Listen

Pope Francis begins, "What gave rise to Mary's act of going to visit her relative Elizabeth? A word of God's angel. Elizabeth in her old age has also conceived a son (see Luke 1:36). Mary knew how to listen to God. But be careful: it was not merely 'hearing' a superficial word, but it was 'listening,' that consists of attention, acceptance and availability to God."[2]

Bl. Anne Catherine Emmerich said when Mary received the Word of God at the annunciation, she was alone in silence, praying for the promised Messiah. Mary is attentive and available, and she accepts God's answer to her prayers through her yes of cooperation: she receives the person of his Word.

Is "listening" simply reading the scriptures? If I read passage after passage, book after book, of the Bible and did not discern God as a person and adjust my life to what I have heard, can it truly be said of me that I have prayed? Of course not. By Mary's example, we see that listening to the Word of God involves not just engaging that Word in our minds—we must allow it to penetrate and move our hearts, until we give it life by bringing its meaning forth in action.

Observe

Pope Francis continues, "Mary also listens to the events, that is, she is . . . attentive to the meaning. This is also true in our life: listening to God who speaks to us, and listening also to daily reality, paying attention to people, to events, because the Lord is at the door of our life and knocks in many ways, he puts signs on our path; he gives us the ability to see them. Mary is the mother of listening, of attentive listening to God and of equally attentive listening to the events of life."[3]

Mary listens in deliberate silence—the language of God. She observes the circumstances and relationships in her life through the Word of God she hears. She ponders the meaning of that Word in his presence and rises to obey it. Mary's simple, daily routine is ripe with observance, pregnant with life and meaning.

Jesus also followed this template for listening to God by observing the events and circumstances of his life. He sought secluded spaces to consider how and where and in whom the Father was working, and he joined him there. "Truly, truly, I say to you, the Son can do nothing of his own accord, but only what he sees the Father doing; for whatever he does, that the Son does likewise. For the Father loves the Son, and shows him all that he himself is doing" (Jn 5:19–20).

Am I available to God's Word every morning or distracted through activity, noise, and lack of discipline? Do I read it and hear it with a heart that searches for him in my relationships and circumstances, or am I just pushing through it to check it off my list?

Where will the Word that I read this morning connect with my circumstances, relationships, habits, and desires today? Do I obey that Word when I observe its perspective on my life?

Verbalize

When our mother of listening receives a whisper of a Word from God in her morning prayer, she hugs the secret close, and it is incarnated. On her way to obey what she has heard and interpreted, Mary prays back to God her understanding of his Word. Her excitement, her awe, her humility, her bliss at being included in such a glorious way in his sweeping, saving plan for all of history is preserved forever in the Church's scripture and liturgy.

"He who sings prays twice," St. Augustine said. The Word of God that Mary has listened to and observed erupts from her in the Magnificat. This is Mary's song. Hers is the song of the whole Church.

Entrust

As Mary entrusts her heart to God in LOVE, he entrusts his Word to her, and she gives birth to that Word in the world, entrusting him to me and you.

At the wedding in Cana, too, Mary brings the Word of God to bear on the practical events and problems of her day and evening. She observes the difficulty of a young married couple at whose wedding feast the wine runs out; she thinks about it.

She knows the Word intimately; to him she verbalizes the problem; she entrusts it fully to him: "They have no wine" (Jn 2:3). Mary listens, she observes, she verbalizes, she entrusts, and a miracle occurs.

Where is God at work in the circumstances and problems in my life? C. S. Lewis said, "Pain is God's megaphone to a deaf world."[4] Where is my pain? Could he be at work there?

In what matter or relationship does he want my cooperation? What do the daily readings say about that today?

In a Nutshell

LOVE: Listen, Observe, Verbalize, and Entrust. As I go to him in the scriptures on a daily basis, I can use this helpful acronym to discern his activity and will and listen, there, to his voice. Like Mary, I observe my relationships and circumstances and how they connect to the Word I receive.

I verbalize back to God my thoughts and fears and feelings about all of it, what response I think he desires from me, what I believe he wants me to do. And I fully entrust all that concerns me to him.

When I LOVE the Word the way Mary teaches me to, the scriptures come alive in my reality the way they did for her. "The word of God is living and active" (Heb 4:12). She, with all of "his servant Israel," knows that God is always speaking. In the beginning he spoke, and it was. Actually, perhaps he *sang*, and "it"—all of everything that is—was.

Song of Songs

Creation is said to have occurred in song (see Job 38:6–7). God himself sings and dances ("rejoices") over his people in a new, spiritual creation (see Zephaniah 3:17). One of my favorite artistic renderings of this beautiful reality is found in *The Magician's Nephew,* the sixth book in C. S. Lewis's Chronicles of Narnia series, where we meet young Polly Plummer, who with her friend Digory Kirke witnesses Aslan create Narnia . . . with a song. Long, sustained notes conjured up beautiful fir trees, lighter ones caused primroses to burst into bloom. Lewis writes, "Thus, with an unspeakable thrill, [Polly] felt quite certain that all the things were coming (as she said) 'out of the Lion's head.' When you listened to his song you heard the thing he was making up: when you looked round you, you saw them."[5]

The Bible contains a rich history of wisdom literature of which song is prominent. The word *psalm* literally means "song." Since "all scripture is inspired by God" (2 Tm 3:16), the psalms were inspired and in some way composed by the Holy Spirit. The psalmist says that all creation sings praise simply by being what it was made to be (19:1–4).

There's a strange little book in the Bible situated within the wisdom section of the Old Testament. In the Song of Solomon, the first verse reads, "The Song of Songs." Similar in language to holy of holies, which means the holiest of holies, the Song of Solomon is the song of all songs, or the most beautiful of songs.

That the Holy Spirit would communicate through a song and take care to emphasize its superlative nature is telling, I believe. A ballad about the intimate relationship between the richest king to ever rule Israel and a common girl, it is poetic and explicit in its expressions of desire and cloaked in a lyrical aura of mystery and need: "You have ravished my heart with a glance of your eyes" (4:9); and, "I am my beloved's and my beloved is mine" (6:3).

If you have ever read it and wondered why this corny little book is in the Bible, read it again with the knowledge that God has written you a song of adoration, filling it full of the same metaphors he uses for himself elsewhere in the scriptures: a shepherd, a banner, paradise, the rock, myrrh, a king, the mountain, living water, and fire. An intimate relationship between God the lover and his beloved soul is about a love as "strong as death" (8:6).

What kind of love is this? It must, in some way, include a profound intimacy, for the context of this song is marital intimacy between the king and the common girl. The mystic saints and doctors of prayer, particularly St. John of the Cross, say this song illustrates the oneness and fulfillment God intends for his relationship with the soul—that is, with you. The first consummation of a marriage is sex, but more than skin on skin, it is the two becoming one, as much spiritual mystery as physical fact (see Ephesians 5:22–32).

The language of the scriptures is startlingly earthy, raw, and splendid. The Bible uses the word *know* for physical intimacy: "Now Adam knew Eve his wife, and she conceived and bore Cain, saying, 'I have gotten a man with the help of the Lord. . . .' Cain knew his wife, and she conceived and bore Enoch" (Gn 4:1, 17).

It means a total and intimate knowing, a comingling of desire, longing, fulfillment, and spirit. God Almighty, the Creator of galaxies, souls, elephants, and atoms, longs for you to acquaint yourself with him and explore his depths in the most vulnerable and intimate of ways.

The terms with which the Holy Spirit describes intimacy with the soul in the Song of Solomon, this choice of language, communicates something shocking about how uncivilized yet approachable he is. The scriptures, the

mystical literature of the saints, and the teachings of the
Church have always maintained that the marriage relationship is illustrative of God's relationship to his people.

The goal, Jesus said, is the two, you and God, becoming one: "The glory which thou hast given me I have
given to them, that they may be one even as we are one, I
in them and thou in me, that they may be perfectly one, so
that the world may know that thou hast sent me and hast
loved them even as thou hast loved me" (Jn 17:22–23).
This spiritual intimacy is what perfects, completes, and/
or consummates us. It is a participation in the glory of
God.

He wants you to want him. He wants you to be hungry for him and his love. He desires that you escape from
the embrace of self and offer yourself—your neediness,
weakness, emptiness—to him, even to the separation of
the joints and marrow of your soul (see Hebrews 4:12).
Your truest, most vulnerable, and most hidden self must
be open to his love, reaching unreservedly to him from
out of the deepest wells of your heart, applauding his
strength, beauty, and intelligence. He asks that you seek
an unspeakable familiarity with him as that of a spouse,
such that there is always something to say, nothing to
hide, perfect comfort, acceptance, profound touch.

Yet he does not bless us with this intimate communion for its own sake. This expression of intimacy and
pleasure is also necessary for the generation of new life.
God told Abram, "I will bless you . . . so that you will
be a blessing" (Gn 12:2). He blesses us so we can spiritually multiply: "Then God blessed them, and God said
to them, 'Be fruitful and multiply'" (Gn 1:28). Part of
God's blessing on Adam and Eve was the pleasure of
physical intimacy and procreation. In the Church's Order
of Celebrating Matrimony, it is said that this marriage

relationship is the only blessing left undestroyed by Eden's catastrophe and Noah's flood, so that physical intimacy and procreation continue as part of God's blessing from the foundation of the world. In Mary and Jesus, it has been spiritually restored.

Do you dare to risk vulnerability in the effort to find God in this world of cynics and scoffers? Every soul who has heard the lover sing to him the loveliest of songs has felt their ridicule: "What is your beloved more than another beloved?" (Sg 5:9).

Though we attempt to answer, the heart is barely able to write the words on our lips, for God is inexplicable, wild, and dangerous, a fathomless mystery. Yet Jesus warns us not to stand on the fringes of intimacy with him: "And then I will declare to them, 'I never *knew* you; depart from me, you evildoers'" (Mt 7:23, emphasis added). We must fall into the bed of faith, ready to be known by the truth, each one alone with God, yet all furiously alive with an eternal song.

St. Peter Julian Eymard said that Mary's interior life consisted especially in love for her divine son. Song of Solomon 8:10 states, "Then I was in his eyes as one who brings peace." Peace means consummation in this context. Only Jesus can satisfy your soul, and the secret is found in his song of love for you (see Song of Solomon 8:6, 10).

Mary knows. Throughout the liturgy of the Church, particularly on Marian feast days, excerpts from the Song of Solomon are applied to her.[6] Mary understood this song; she experienced it, and it moved her to sing her own. But even more than that, she became a song.

O God, Beyond All Praising

Although I don't usually put much stock in near-death experiences, one account has stayed with me because of how it ties to this idea of God's love song for us. In his book *In Heaven*, Dean Braxton relates:

> The next thing I saw was one of the beings before the Throne rising up from a kneeling position. This being rose up like an elevator rising up from the bottom floor to the top slowly. . . . It was a good hundred stories or higher. When it reached its highest point, this being rose its arms over its head to the full extent and extended its fingers out wide. . . . After this being had finished rising, it opened its mouth and broke the silence that was taking place. It started to sing in a language I understood but knew was not an earthly language. This language seemed to be this being's own language, but I understood it. The sound that came out of its mouth was beautiful and yet, just one note. It came from the innermost part of its being. . . . I could see the notes coming out of the being's mouth. They had substance to them. . . . You could hold them and walk on them. You could hear and experience each note that came out of this being's mouth.
>
> This being kept singing and producing music until it filled the atmosphere with the sound of these notes. These notes finally ended up entering the Father on the Throne. . . . When this being finally reached an apex or top of praise, the being stopped and bowed back on it knees, like slowly going down in an elevator.[7]

Braxton went on to describe how every being and creation in heaven had its own unique, particular song so that all of heaven throbbed with worship. Each being's song went into God and came out of God in an continuous exchange of praise and love that was intimate and unique yet as interconnected as a symphony.

I immediately recognized the similarities between the Psalms, the Song of Solomon, Mary's Magnificat, and what this angel and God were offering one another.

I finished and laid the book aside, astounded at the glory of what I had read, but I also felt somewhat bereft. I sat there in tears for long moments and prayed desperately, *Lord, what is my song? What is the song I sing to you and that you sing to me? What can I sing for you now and throughout all eternity?*

I wept harder than perhaps I have in my whole life when he answered me: "Sonja, you *are* the song."

You Are the Song

Most of us think of the Magnificat as something Mary said or sang. But Mary doesn't sing a song that magnifies the Lord. Mary *is* the song. Mary *is* the Magnificat.

And you are meant to be a magnificat, too, just by being who you are meant to be: your personality, temperament, duties, and station in life, minus sin.

Mary affirms that we, too, can grow fuller and fuller of the Holy Spirit, who engorges us with himself so that we become all that was in God's mind and heart for us at our creation. Her Magnificat invites us to that fullness, she invites us to *be* a magnificat with her, and she shows us the way to do it.

The more we clear away the sin; the more lowly and hungry we allow and discipline ourselves to be; the more we prevail upon the new ark and his mercy seated there;

the more we are in the scriptures listening for his Word, the more he shows the strength of his arm.

Mary was made for God himself; her every endowment was for his pleasure and plan and disposal. She tells us through her Magnificat that she is who she is, not because of anything she did but simply because of grace. And that grace abounded to her in such fullness that the archangel from heaven's throne praised her. St. Catherine of Siena experienced this exactly when God said to her, "You are she who is not; whereas I am He who is."[8] And then God "sang" to St. Catherine: "Even your own existence comes not from yourself but from me, for I loved you before you came into being."[9]

Mary carried—contained in her immaculate womb—the God whom all creation cannot contain. Truly it is right that we call her blessed with the scriptures, for she brought the world a unique relationship with God: the possibility of carrying him within us and to others. While such elevated language might puzzle or even offend some brothers and sisters, as Bl. Columbia Marion pointed out, "To separate Christ from His Mother is to divide Christ. . . . Where the Mother is left out, the Son is no longer understood."[10]

Mary invites us through her Magnificat to hear God speak "as he spoke to our fathers" and to her, indeed to all the people of the Bible and Church history. God always keeps his promises; we just don't know what they are because we are not in the scriptures consistently. Mary teaches us how to love the Word the way she does so that all of us lowly ones can experience the wonder of God's promises and their powerful fulfillment in our own lives.

The Magnificat is the fruit of Mary's prayer and model of prayer for the Church. But Mary magnified the Lord, not because of the words she said or sang in praise of him but because she fulfilled God's purpose for her to the fullest possible degree. Mary fully realized her potential through the Holy Spirit, and in so doing, her whole life was a song that magnified the Lord. Mary does not sing the Magnificat. Mary *is* the Magnificat. Like her, my life and being are a song from God's heart that he sings to me every second of my existence, one that he longs for me to grow into fully, a song I can sing back to him for all eternity.

Like Mary, you *are* the song.

Let's Review

- The imagery of the wisdom literature, particularly the Song of Solomon, *reveals the longing of God to be one* with us, *in intimate union with us.*
- *This intimacy is necessary* not simply for pleasure, but to produce new life in us and others.
- By surrendering to this Song of Solomon and recognizing the invitation to divine intimacy, *Mary did not just sing the Magnificat, she* became *a Magnificat,* a living song of praise.
- *Mary's Magnificat is an invitation from the Holy Spirit* to become a magnificat, too.
- *Mary shows that God will give you the desires of your heart when you receive and obey his Word,* holding nothing back.
- *God is always extending mercy* in order to draw us into the closest possible relationship with him.
- *If you are in the scriptures on a daily basis, you will hear God speak* to your relationships and circumstances.
- Like Mary, *you are a magnificat.*

Invitation

Mary's Magnificat is her invitation to be a magnificat, too. Her name, from the root *myrrh*, illustrates her unique obedience and suffering for love with Christ for the redemption of the human race that became part of her song; she invites each of us to offer the same in our own ways, through our own personalities and temperaments, within our own duties and stations and circumstances.

But we can never do this on our own. God did not choose Mary because of her humility; Mary was humble because God chose her. God equips those whom he calls. We may feel our magnificat is too hard, hidden, insignificant, or small, but she shows us that when we rely on her weapons of prayer, scripture, and humility, God will do great things for us, too: if we are not exalted here on earth, certainly we will be in heaven.

Like her, my own being becomes more magnificat as often as I call on the name of the Lord and wait for him to provide miraculously in my life and the less I am weakened by sin. He exalts those who are humble enough to imitate her example and allow God to bring the song in his heart for them to fruition, to be sung back to him in full-throated thanksgiving for all eternity. Let us pray.

God Prompt–LOVE the Word

L | Listen

"The heavens are telling the glory of God; and the firmament proclaims his handiwork. Day to day pours forth speech, and night to night declares knowledge. There is no speech, nor are there words; their voice is not heard;

yet their voice goes out through all the earth, and their words to the end of the world" (Ps 19:1–4).

O | *Observe*

Study carefully these verses of praise, themselves a song, like the Magnificat.

Who and what is this psalm about?
Where and when does this song take place?
Why and how is praise occurring?

V | *Verbalize*

Who, what, where, when, why, and how do you want to thank and praise God for right now?

E | *Entrust*

Lord, you are my beloved, and I am yours . . . there is no higher praise than this . . . Hallelujah.

Notes

1. Blessed Is She Who Believed

1. Thomas Aquinas, *Summa Theologica* 2-2.29.

2. Emmerich is reported to have borne on her own body, as have many of the saints, the mystical wounds of Christ; St. Paul seems to refer to this condition in Galatians 6:17.

3. These patterns of prayer later formed the basis of the Divine Office of the Church.

4. Herbert Thurston, "Symbolism," *The Catholic Encyclopedia*, vol. 14 (New York: Robert Appleton Company, 1912), accessed October 23, 2018, http://www.newadvent.org/cathen/14373b.htm.

5. Cornelius à Lapide on Galatians, chap. 4, *Patristic Bible Commentary*, accessed March 25, 2019, https://sites.google.com/site/aquinas-studybible/home/galatians/cornelius-a-lapide-on-galatians/chapter-1/chapter-2/chapter-3/chapter-4.

6. Lapide on Galatians, chap. 4.

7. Particularly the Mass readings for Catholics. See *Magnificat* or *Word Among Us* magazines; http://universalis.com or http://www.usccb.org/readings; or the Laudate or iBreviary phone apps.

8. Sonja Corbitt, *How to Pray Like Mary* (West Chester, PA: Ascension Press, 2020).

2. And Mary Said . . .

1. Nissan Mindel, "Miriam," Chabad, accessed February 15, 2019, https://www.chabad.org/library/article_cdo/aid/112396/jewish/Miriam.htm.

2. Miriam's name, meaning "bitterness," can also be translated as "rebellious."

3. Later, these women were given the specific designation *myrrhophore* for this service.

4. Thomas Aquinas, *Catena Aurea: The Gospel of St. Luke*, vol. 2, pt. 1 (New York: Costmo Classics, 2007), 42.

5. "In the Greek translation of the Old Testament, the ineffable Hebrew name YHWH, by which God revealed himself to Moses, is rendered as *Kyrios*, 'Lord.' From then on, 'Lord' becomes the more usual name by which to indicate the divinity of Israel's God. The New Testament uses this full sense of the title 'Lord' both for the Father and—what is new—for Jesus, who is thereby recognized as God Himself" (CCC 446).

6. Cornelius à Lapide, *The Great Commentary of Cornelius à Lapide*, vol. 4 (London: John Hodges, 1887), 44.

7. Augustine, "Of Holy Virginity," trans. C. L. Cornis, in *Nicene and Post-Nicene Fathers*, 1st ser., vol. 3, ed. Philip Schaff (Buffalo, NY: Christian Literature Publishing, 1887); rev. and ed. Kevin Knight, New Advent, accessed February 4, 2019, http://www.newadvent.org/fathers/1310.htm.

3. For He Has Regarded the Low Estate of His Handmaiden

1. Caryll Houselander, *The Reed of God* (Notre Dame, IN: Ave Maria Press, 2006), 33.

2. Jake Tawney, "Veiling in the Liturgy," Catholic Stand, March 13, 2013, http://www.catholicstand.com/veiling-in-the-liturgy.

3. Cornelius à Lapide, *Great Commentary of Cornelius à Lapide*, vol. 4 (London: John Hodges, 1887), 48.

4. Popularly attributed to Dominican preacher Henri-Dominique Lacordaire. "Rosary Quotes that Will Knock Your Socks Off," Heroic Families, February 9, 2018, http://heroicfamilies.com/2018/02/09/rosary-quotes-that-will-knock-your-socks-off.

4. He . . . Has Done Great Things for Me

1. Martin Luther, "The Works of Martin Luther, Magnificat—Translated and Explained 1520-1," BibleExplore.com, accessed February 4, 2019, http://www.godrules.net/library/luther/NEW1luther_c5.htm.

2. See my book *How to Pray Like Mary* for the full story, the science behind the use of art therapy, and the specifics on the exercise that revealed my issue.

3. Thomas Aquinas, *Summa Theologica* 1.25.6.4; retrieved from New Advent, February 16, 2019, http://www.newadvent.org/summa/1025.htm#article6.

4. Hesychius, Bishop of Jerusalem (hom. 2 de S. Maria), Lapide commentary on Luke 1:49.

5. See biblestudyevangelista.com or Amazon.com for the Mary journal.

5. His Mercy Is on Those Who Fear Him

1. Francis, *Urbi et Orbi Message*, Libreria Editrice Vaticana, March 31, 2013, http://w2.vatican.va/content/francesco/en/messages/urbi/documents/papa-francesco_20130331_urbi-et-orbi-pasqua.html.

2. Frances J. Crosby, "He Hideth My Soul," published 1890, public domain.

3. Hippolytus, "Second Fragment of the Visions of Daniel and Nebuchadnezzar, Saying One," trans. S. D. F. Salmond, in *Ante-Nicene Fathers*, vol. 5, ed. Alexander Roberts, James Donaldson, and A. Cleveland Coxe (Buffalo, NY: Christian Literature Publishing, 1886); rev. and ed. Kevin Knight, New Advent, accessed December 1, 2018, http://www.newadvent.org/fathers/0502.htm.

4. *The Works of Gregory Thaumaturgus, Dionysius of Alexandria, and Archelaus: Translations of the Writings of the Fathers*, ed. Alexander Roberts and James Donaldson (Edinburgh: T and T Clark, 1875), 123.

5. John Henry Newman, "The Times of Antichrist, Lecture 1," in *The Patristical Idea of Antichrist*, The National Institute for Newman Studies, accessed December 3, 2018, http://www.newmanreader.org/works/arguments/antichrist/lecture1.html.

6. He Has Shown Strength with His Arm

1. W. H. Vanstone, *The Stature of Waiting* (Harrisburg, PA: Morehouse, 2006).

2. Thomas Aquinas, *Catena Aurea*, Luke 22:15, quoting St. Bede, Dominican House of Studies, accessed July 31, 2019, https://dhspriory.org/thomas/english/CALuke.htm#22.

7. He Has Put Down … and Exalted

1. Augustine, "The Replacement of the Fallen Angels by Elect Men," in *Handbook on Faith, Hope, and Love*, trans. Albert C. Outler, Christian Classics Ethereal Library, accessed February 16, 2019, http://www.ccel.org/ccel/augustine/enchiridion.chapter9.html.

2. Cyril, homily on Luke 1, Thomas Aquinas, *Catena Aurea*, electronic e-Sword.

3. Benedict XVI, Homily of His Holiness Pope Benedict XVI, Libreria Editrice Vaticana, August 21, 2005, http://w2.vatican.va/content/benedict-xvi/en/homilies/2005/documents/hf_ben-xvi_hom_20050821_20th-world-youth-day.html.

8. He Has Filled the Hungry

1. Augustine, *The Expositions on the Psalms*, trans. Alexander Cleveland Coxe, vol. 2 (Scotts Valley, CA: CreateSpace, 2017), 208.

2. Richard A. McCormick, "Notes on Moral Theology," *Theological Studies* 34, no. 1 (February 1973): 53–102, https://doi.org/10.1177/004056397303400104.

3. James Brodrick, *Robert Bellarmine: Saint and Scholar* (Westminster, MD: Newman Press, 1961), 170.

4. Alban Butler, *Lives of the Saints*, vol. 4, 76.

5. Alban Butler, *Lives of the Saints*, vol. 3, 362.

6. Alphonsus Liguori, *The True Spouse of Jesus Christ* (West Monroe, LA: St. Athanasius Press, 2014) 183, 184.

7. Raymond of Capua, *The Life of Saint Catherine of Siena* (Charlotte, NC: Tan Books, 2011), 135.

9. He Has Helped His Servant Israel

1. Scott Hahn, *A Father Who Keeps His Promises: God's Covenant Love in Scripture* (Cincinnati, OH: Servant, 1998).

2. John Paul II, "The Root of Anti-Judaism in the Christian Environment," Vatican.va, April 13, 1986, http://www.vatican.va/jubilee_2000/magazine/documents/ju_mag_01111997_p-42x_en.html.

3. Lapide on Matthew, chap. 27.

4. "Christ Assumed Flesh, Conceived and Born of the Virgin," in *The Apostolic Fathers with Justin Martyr and Irenaeus*, Christian Classics Ethereal Library, accessed December 31, 2018, http://www.ccel.org/ccel/schaff/anf01.ix.iv.xxiii.html.

5. John Chrysostom, *Homily in Matthew ii*, St. Thomas Aquinas Catena electronic e-Sword.

10. As He Spoke to Our Fathers

1. Benedict XVI, "On the Solemnity of the Assumption of the Blessed Virgin Mary," Libreria Editrice Vaticana, August 15, 2005, http://w2.vatican.va/content/benedict-xvi/en/homilies/2005/documents/hf_ben-xvi_hom_20050815_assunzione-maria.html.

2. Francis, "Recital of the Rosary for the Conclusion of the Marian Month of May," Libreria Editrice Vaticana, May 31, 2013, http://w2.vatican.va/content/francesco/en/speeches/2013/may/documents/papa-francesco_20130531_conclusione-mese-mariano.html.

3. Francis, "Recital of the Rosary."

4. C. S. Lewis, *The Problem of Pain* (San Francisco: HarperOne, 2003), 93.

5. C. S. Lewis, *The Magician's Nephew* (New York: HarperCollins, 1955), 115–16.

6. *Tota pulchra es*, or "You are completely beautiful," is one of the five antiphons for the psalms of Second Vespers for the feast of the Immaculate Conception. Referring to the Virgin Mary, the prayer speaks of her Immaculate Conception, with some of its text quoted from the book of Judith and others from Song of Songs, such as 4:7.

7. Dean Braxton, *In Heaven* (Maitland, FL: Xulon Press, 2009), 128–31.

8. Raymond of Capua, *The Life of St. Catherine of Siena: The Classic on Her Life and Accomplishments as Recorded by Her Spiritual Director* (Charlotte, NC: TAN Books, 2003), 55.

9. Catherine of Siena, *The Dialogue* (Mahwah, NJ: Paulist Press, 1980), 29.

10. Columba Marmion, *Christ the Life of the Soul* (Tacoma, WA: Angelico Press, 2012), 339–40.

Sonja Corbitt is a Catholic author and speaker who has produced several multimedia Bible studies, including *Unleashed, Fearless, Ignite,* and *Fulfilled.* She also created LOVE the Word Bible study method.

A Carolina native who was raised as a Southern Baptist, Corbitt attended Mitchell College and the Southern Baptist Seminary Extension before converting to Catholicism. She has since served as director of religious education at St. John Vianney Catholic Church in Gallatin, Tennessee, and as executive director of Risen Radio in Lebanon, Tennessee.

Corbitt is the host of *Bible Study Evangelista Show* on radio and podcast. She is in formation as a Third Order Carmelite. Corbitt is a columnist at *The Great Adventure Bible Study* blog and a contributor to *Magnificat.* Her book / Bible study *Unleashed* was featured as a thirteen-part series on CatholicTV.

She lives in Tennessee with her husband, Bob, and their two sons.

biblestudyevangelista.com
Facebook: sonjacorbitt
Instagram: @biblestudyevangelista
Pinterest: bibleevangelista

MORE BOOKS BY
Sonja Corbitt

Unleashed
How to Receive Everything the Holy Spirit Wants to Give You

Sonja Corbitt was an evangelical Baptist before converting to Catholicism. In *Unleashed*, she shares her passion for the scriptures by weaving the Word of God with her own experiences to show readers how the Holy Spirit flows through their lives in relationships, prayer, and times of suffering.

Fearless
Conquer Your Demons and Love with Abandon

What are the sources of anxiety, stress, and fear you experience in your life?

Popular Catholic speaker and author Sonja Corbitt believes that these often-paralyzing emotions are the direct result of our everyday battles against sin and temptation. In *Fearless*, she equips us with the spiritual tools we need to restore our spiritual well-being.

Find more resources from Sonja Corbitt at biblestudyevangelista.com